IDENTIFYING

BARBIE® DOLLS

The new compact study guide and identifier

IDENTIFYING

BARBIE® DOLLS

The new compact study guide and identifier

Janine Fennick

CHARTWELL
BOOKS, INC.

A QUINTET BOOK

Published by Chartwell Books
A Division of Book Sales, Inc.
114, Northfield Avenue
Edison, New Jersey 08837

ISBN 0-7858-0869-8

This book was designed and produced by
Quintet Publishing Limited
6 Blundell Street
London N7 9BH

Creative Director: Richard Dewing
Art Director: Silke Braun
Designer: Rod Teasdale
Project Editor: Clare Hubbard
Editor: Rosie Hankin
Photography: Garry Stuart

Typeset in Great Britain by
Central Southern Typesetters, Eastbourne
Manufactured in Singapore
by Eray Scan Pte Ltd
Printed in Singapore
by Star Standard Industries Pte Ltd

CONTENTS

ACKNOWLEDGMENTS

I'd like to thank all those people who have motivated me and encouraged me during the completion of this project: my parents, Cynthia and Manny Fennick; Michael Macomber, Eric Bayrd, John Copeland, Donna Datre, Carole DiSalvo, Tim Earls, Gail Falotico, Jim Faroane, Neil Gaiman, Nancy Hutchins, Jennifer Adams and Miss Valerie Kelley, Monique Kromer, Julie and Al Melle, Sharon Perez-Abreu, Laurel Sutton, Gwyn Wright, and all the other significant people too numerous to mention.

My undying gratitude goes to Bruce Adams, Linda Oliva, Rose Rothaar, and Frank Sposato for the loan of so many wonderful dolls and A. Glenn Mandeville, Lloyd McMillon, Dan Petrolati, Benita Schwartz, Judy Traina, Mary Winder, Barbara Whitton Berger, and Richard Withington for their support and accolades.

Last but not least, my heartfelt thanks to Tonya Holly and the members of the Tennessee River Valley Barbie® Doll Collectors Club, especially for all their southern hospitality!

INTRODUCTION

Collecting Barbie® dolls is one of the most popular hobbies today. However, whether you are collecting for nostalgia's sake or for a potential investment, the field of collectible Barbie® dolls can be pretty intimidating, especially for new collectors just getting in on the fun. Mattel has been producing dolls since 1959 and there are hundreds to choose from. So how can you tell one Barbie® doll from another? How do you know how old she is? And what about all her friends and relatives?

That's where this book comes in—to help you identify the different faces and

phases of the Barbie® doll and her friends from 1959 to the present. This book has been organized in a chronological fashion and discusses the Barbie® doll herself as well as her friends and family members. The Ponytail Era focuses on dolls produced from 1959 through 1966, the Mod Era from 1967 through 1972, and the Collectible Era from 1973 through the present. The best way to maneuver yourself through the world of Barbie® dolls is to learn as much as possible. Read as many reference books as you can find, take notes, and keep them with you while shopping at doll shows, flea markets, or in

Group shot of Mod Era Barbie® dolls.

doll stores. If possible, find a local Barbie® doll collectors club in your area and give them a call. If you're fortunate enough to own a computer, there are many different avenues to connect with Barbie® doll collectors around the world, including discussion forums on all the commercial online services and a multitude of websites to explore. Knowledge is your best weapon against being duped. You should keep in mind that not everyone claiming to be an expert is one.

HINTS AND TIPS ON COLLECTING

The most important considerations in any form of collecting, including Barbie® dolls, are your personal budget and amount of storage space. Obviously, your first impulse is to buy every doll you come across. However, unless you're a multi-millionaire with a mansion, this isn't going to be possible. Remember, Mattel has produced Barbie® dolls for the last 39 years and even the most enthusiastic Barbie® collector doesn't love them all.

In my opinion, the best collecting strategy is to focus on one or two areas that you think you might like the best. Is it the vintage dolls (from the Ponytail Era, 1959 through 1966), the Mod Era (1967 through 1972), or more recent collectible editions? Do you only like redheads or

Barbie® doll Milk Chocolates from Canada, 1997.

African-American dolls? Your collection can even be centered around a specific theme such as music, careers, or the color blue. It all depends on what appeals to you, and you alone.

Once you've made a choice on collection content, the next consideration is condition. Items range from "Never Removed From Box" (commonly known as "NRFB") to destroyed. There are two distinct groups of collectors—those who want their dolls in pristine condition, never taken out of the original packaging and those who prefer things that have been taken out of the package because it is easier to redress and display them. However, items in mint condition will always command the

highest prices. The newest breed of Barbie®
doll collectors tend to purchase NRFB
items for investment purposes. However
most new collectible Barbie® dolls do not
appreciate in value significantly, especially if
Mattel responds to collector demands and
creates higher production runs than initially
expected. Therefore, the best advice I can
give is "Buy what you like and enjoy it!"

BUYING BARBIE® DOLLS

Now that you've decided how you're
going to form your collection and the
areas that you want to concentrate on, it's
time to make your first purchase. Buying
your dolls in a department or toy store is

*Barbie® Sings! record set—a specially packaged set
of three 45rpm records from 1961 featuring six
songs sung by Barbie® and Ken®.*

easy. However if you are planning to buy
through mail-order, the Internet, or at doll
or toy shows, there are a few things to
look out for.

DOLL SHOWS

If you buy at a doll show, you are entitled to
ask questions and check the doll that you

only car designed for the *Barbie®* and *Ken®* T.M. teenage dolls

Barbie's® Own Sports Car in original packaging, produced by Irwin Products in 1962.

want to buy. However you should ask the dealer before touching or opening anything. The price should be marked on the doll as should any information about repairs. You can ask for a discount. However, if a dealer says his prices are firm, please don't argue the point. You should also shop around and compare prices before you purchase, as dealers are entitled to determine their own prices. Most dealers will hold an item for you so that you can look around before finally purchasing. However if you change your mind and decide you do not want the doll, it is courteous to inform the dealer. You can pay for merchandise at a doll show with cash or checks. Some dealers accept credit cards, but you should check this before you attempt to buy. You are entitled to a written receipt. If you are in a state that charges sales tax, be prepared to pay it.

MAIL ORDER AND ONLINE SALES

Buying items through mail order or online is more problematic because you are buying the merchandise unseen. Ask other collectors about the mail order companies that they use and check back issues of magazines and ad papers to see

---

Useful Terms

NRFB—Never Removed From Box— means the doll or fashion is still in its original box or sewn on its original card with all original packaging intact.
MIB—Mint in Box—means the doll or fashion is in pristine condition and has its original package but may have been taken out of packaging at some point.
TNT—Twist 'n Turn™.
Pak—budget mix-and-match garments that were sold separately.
Vintage—usually refers to Mattel dolls and outfits issued between 1959 and 1972.

---

which dealers have advertised for a long period of time. If the items that you are buying are new or have never been removed from the box these sales should be straightforward and problem-free. Loose or vintage merchandise is more difficult, as one person's assessment of the condition of an item isn't necessarily the same as another's. For this reason it is standard procedure for a dealer to grant the buyer a five to seven day return privilege. Be sure to inform the company that you are returning the item as some will not accept returns if they have not been properly notified in advance.

As for doll shows, the responsibility for comparison shopping before you do a deal is yours. In addition, double check that you are being charged the correct price plus the addition of shipping costs and/or applicable taxes. Check your order carefully when it arrives and if there are any problems, contact the dealer immediately. Most reputable dealers will attempt to rectify problems amicably.

CLEANING AND RESTORATION HINTS

There is no one perfect way to clean and restore Barbie® dolls. The methods listed below are my own personal preferences based on recommendations from other collectors and trial and error experimen-

Collection of fashion booklets.

tation. You may discover that none of these are satisfactory or something else works better. In any case, please be advised that I cannot take responsibility for any results you may obtain. Therefore, it is suggested that you test these and any other methods on "basket-case" dolls first.

Since Barbie® dolls are made of plastic, many modern household products can be used in clean-up situations. The best place to start is to soak dolls in a tub filled with a mild liquid detergent and warm water.

This will loosen the dirt relatively easily. Synthetic "scrubbies" used for washing non-stick cookware are exceptionally good for scouring off ground-in grime because they don't scratch or take off face paint. For really filthy dolls, I've found that Castrol® Super Clean, an automotive cleaner/degreaser, works wonders without taking off face or nail paint. However, read the instructions carefully and wear latex gloves when using this product as it is very strong.

BRUNETTE #3 PONYTAIL IN SOLO IN THE SPOTLIGHT, STOCK #982, WITH PINK SILHOUETTE BOX, CIRCA 1960.

This type of box is a rare find. Dolls were given to toy stores in this kind of packaging as display items and are quite sought after by collectors.

Doll, box, and outfit courtesy of Linda Oliva.

Ink stains can be removed by using over-the-counter acne products such as Clearasil or Oxy 10 blemish cream. The "Vanishing" Formula works best. Apply a thick coat directly on the stain and then place the doll in strong sunlight. Over the course of the next few days, continue to check the spot and reapply the cream until the ink disappears. However, this should not be used on face paint, which can fade.

Doll's hair can be washed using the same methods as your own, a mild shampoo followed by a good conditioner. Conditioner should remain on badly matted hair for a longer period of time. After rinsing, gently comb out all knots and snarls with a fine-toothed comb. Commercial hair gels or mousses can be applied to aid in setting. Pipe cleaners, toothpicks, or Barbie® doll-sized curlers can be used to set hairstyles.

Use orthodontic rubber bands to replace broken or disintegrated originals. These can usually be obtained from your own dentist or orthodontist. Occasionally they can also be found at doll shows.

There is nothing currently available to completely remove the green spots that result from the oxidation of the base metal earring pins used on vintage dolls. However, some positive results can be obtained by using a combination of Tarnex Liquid Tarnish Remover and Zud Bathroom Cleanser. First carefully remove the doll's head by placing it in a coffee cup or pan of boiling water until it is soft enough to come off the neck knob. Then, dip a cotton swab in the Tarnex and gently wipe away any green that might have built up on the inside of the ears. Next, mix a few drops of Tarnex with the Zud powder in a glass or plastic dish until a thick paste forms. It should be roughly the consistency of sour cream. Apply the paste to the green spots with a toothpick and let sit. When the paste has completely dried out and can be flaked off, reapply. Avoid getting this on facial paint because it will be ruined. Using this mixture will probably not remove the green entirely but it reduces it significantly. Unfortunately, most Fashion Queen heads do not respond well to this method.

CARING FOR CLOTHING

The first rule of thumb is to treat Barbie® doll clothing in the same manner you would your own, with one important exception—do not put them in the washing machine; wash them by hand. Most cotton fabrics can be washed in regular laundry detergent and colorfast bleach. Test garments for colorfastness before immersing them completely. Believe it or not, even the red plastic buttons on certain outfits can run.

For hard to remove stains, a mixture of one part lemon juice concentrate and one part white vinegar can be applied. Place the garment in strong sunlight and reapply liquid as needed. Rewash in mild detergent and rinse. This method may take a few days to a few weeks depending on the severity of the stain.

JAPANESE SIDE-PART BARBIE® DOLL IN KIMONO, CIRCA 1966.
This is a rare Japanese version of the Side-part Barbie® doll. The Japanese were enthusiastic Barbie® doll collectors even in the early 1960s and had many dolls and outfits exclusively made for their country. This is just one example of the lovely dolls produced for the Japanese market.
Courtesy of Linda Oliva.

Yellowed wedding gowns and other white dresses of delicate fabrics can be whitened by placing them in a flat glass pan, covered with warm water. Drop one to two white denture cleaning tablets into the pan

**PRICE CLUB/COSTCO SILVER ROYALE BARBIE®
DOLL, NEVER REMOVED FROM THE BOX,
CIRCA 1996.**

*One of the most popular dolls released in 1996, the
Silver Royale was an instant hit with collectors
everywhere. Considered a "sleeper," Barbie® doll collectors
liked her for her looks and her reasonable price point.
Unfortunately, she was only available at Price
Club/Costco wholesale warehouse stores which are mainly
located in the Northeastern United States. She sold out
very quickly and secondary market prices skyrocketed,
especially in markets where the stores did not exist, such
as the Southeast.*

and allow them to dissolve completely
(approximately 10 minutes). Turn the dress
over and repeat the process. Rinse, place on
Barbie® doll-sized hangers and allow to dry.
To clean other clothing made of fine fabrics

(especially evening gowns) check with your
local cleaners regarding the possibility of
commercial dry cleaning.

To repair damaged or torn clothing, use
fine thread, thin needles, and original
zippers or snaps if possible. If a garment is
beyond repair, the snaps, buttons, zippers,
or trims can be salvaged for this purpose.

IDENTIFYING FORGERIES

Basically, it is not worth the effort to forge
the average Barbie® doll. Therefore, only
the rarest dolls rank among those where
forgery attempts have been made.
Rerooted hairstyles can be easily spotted
by checking the inside of a doll's scalp.
Mattel used commercial rooting machines
which created a "chain stitch" inside the
head. Rerooting must be done by hand.
This process requires knotting each
individual hair plug separately. Any visible
knots are a dead giveaway. However, if you
suspect a doll has been rerooted, please ask
the owner before popping the doll's head
off. Fragile neck knobs can break and
vinyl heads tear. You don't want to have to
pay for a ruined rare doll if you're wrong.

Repaints can be much harder to spot.
Look for visible brush strokes and lumps,
roughness, or possibly unevenness in the
painting. Examining the doll under a
magnifying glass or a jeweler's loupe can
be quite revealing in this regard.

BARBIE® DOLL IDENTIFIER

GOIN' TO THE GAME BARBIE
MILLICENT ROBERTS FASHION, CIRCA 1996.
This outfit is one of the two initial Barbie® Millicent Roberts outfit releases,
modeled by a Romantic Interlude Barbie® doll.

THE PONYTAIL ERA
1959 – 1966

The original concept of the Barbie® doll was developed in the late 1950s by toy manufacturer Ruth Handler, who along with her husband, Elliot, had founded the Mattel toy company. Inspired by her daughter Barbara's enjoyment of playing with dolls, especially paper dolls, Mrs. Handler decided that the time was right for a teenage fashion doll with a high fashion wardrobe on the American market. Although there had been other fashion dolls produced in the past, the Barbie® doll, named after the Handlers' daughter, would prove to be the most successful one in history.

In February 1959, the very first Barbie® doll made her debut. Despite poor initial interest on the part of toy stores and department-store buyers, the 11½-inch doll billed as a Teen Age Fashion Model became a hit with girls everywhere. Since then, she has undergone a gradual metamorphosis to reflect the

BRUNETTE #1 PONYTAIL BARBIE® DOLL IN PLANTATION BELLE, STOCK #966, CIRCA 1959.
This was the very first Barbie® doll ever produced by Mattel. At the time of her release, she was considered too provocative in looks by store owners, who ordered her in very small quantities.

constant change in standards of beauty, hairstyle, and fashion. In fact, during her first two years of life alone, five different versions of the Barbie® doll were issued.

As a result, there has been much confusion surrounding the identification of early Barbie® dolls. Many adults who played with a Barbie® doll as children assume that *their* first Barbie® doll is *the* first Barbie® doll. Unfortunately, this is generally not the case. The original 1959 Ponytail Barbie® doll (stock #850), or #1 as she is known to collectors, possesses a unique set of distinguishing characteristics.

These include:
★ arched V-shaped eyebrows (earlier dolls will be handpainted, later editions stenciled)
★ vivid red lips and nails (which sometimes may have faded to an orangey red)
★ soft Saran hair styled in a ponytail with a hard curl on the bottom
★ soft curly bangs
★ handpainted black eyes with white irises and thick black eyeliner around the entire eye

BLONDE #1 PONYTAIL BARBIE® DOLL IN EASTER PARADE, STOCK #971, CIRCA 1959.
Not only is the doll a rare find, but so is the outfit she's wearing. Easter Parade was one of the first three outfits ever produced for Barbie® dolls and was only available for one year. The dress was later rereleased by itself as Apple Print Sheath, stock #917.
Doll and outfit courtesy of Linda Oliva.

In addition, there is a round hole in the bottom of each foot filled with a copper metal tube. These fit into two metal prongs protruding from the round black plastic stand that accompanied her. Her body is solid, made of a heavy, rigid plastic which some collectors say has a "waxy" or "crayon" type scent, and may be pale or ivory white. She is jointed at the neck, arms, and legs, which are all completely straight and will not bend. The markings on the right side of the doll's bottom read:

> ★ **Barbie™** ★
> **Pats. Pending**
> **© MCMLVIII**
> **by**
> ★ **Mattel** ★
> **Inc.**

Her accessories included a strapless black and white zebra-striped bathing suit, a pair of black, open-toed, mule-style shoes with holes in the bottom of the soles to accommodate the doll's stand (commonly known as #1 shoes), white cats-eye sunglasses, golden hoop pierced earrings, the black plastic #1 stand, and a fashion

BRUNETTE #3 PONYTAIL BARBIE® DOLL IN RESORT SET, STOCK #963, CIRCA 1960.
Note the change in facial paint between the #1 doll and the #3 doll. Rounder eyebrows, blue eyes, and eyeliner were added in order to give the Barbie® doll a softer, more fresh-faced look. Early Ponytail dolls also have flocking underneath their hair.

booklet. She came in a slim white shoebox-style package illustrated with three colorful bands of Barbie® dolls modeling her *haute couture* clothes.

The second issue, or #2 Ponytail Barbie® is almost identical in appearance to her predecessor, except that there are no holes in her feet and the #1 stand was replaced with a new one consisting of a black wire stand and matching plastic pedestal. Both the #1 and #2 dolls were available with blonde or brunette hair. However, twice as many blondes as brunettes were produced. Although it cannot be proven, the #2 doll seems to be much more elusive than the #1 doll.

The third issue (#3) of the Ponytail Barbie® doll was released in 1960. After extensive marketing studies, Mattel decided to change the doll's hard-looking make-up, to a softer, more fresh-faced look. The #3's distinguishing features include:

★ blue eyes
★ blue or brown eyeliner on upper lids only
★ pale or ivory white skin tone

BLONDE #3 PONYTAIL BARBIE® DOLL IN BARBIE-Q, STOCK #962, CIRCA 1960.
Part of the fun of collecting Barbie® doll outfits is the number of little accessories that accompanied them. This outfit has tiny kitchen utensils, and a pot holder to go along with the dress, apron, and hat. Perfect clothing plus complete accessories will command the highest prices.

19

BRUNETTE #4 PONYTAIL BARBIE® DOLL IN PAK LAMÉ SHEATH, CIRCA 1960. *In addition to outfits, Mattel also released mix-and-match separates on cards, known as Pak items. This gold and navy sheath is just one of many different pieces available throughout the 1960s.*

BLONDE #4 PONYTAIL BARBIE® DOLL IN ENCHANTED EVENING, STOCK #983, CIRCA 1960. *The Barbie® doll had an extensive wardrobe which ran the gamut from casual through elegant. This gown and fur stole is one of the most popular with vintage Barbie® doll collectors.*

She was again available as either a blonde or a brunette styled in a ponytail, although some dolls have been found, that have never been removed from the box, with braided hairstyles. Also some dolls have been found wearing the earlier gold hoop earrings, while others have on pearl studs. Most have the later mule shoes with solid soles but some dolls have been found with #1 shoes instead.

Due to a flaw in the type of vinyl used on the first three issues of the Ponytail Barbie®, the pink skin tone tends to fade to a sickly white or, in some cases, uneven splotches. Mattel was able to correct the problem on the next version of the Barbie® doll, the fourth or #4 Ponytail. The #4 is identical to the #3 in all ways except that she retains her tanned flesh tone, her limbs have a more rubbery feel, and she is only found with blue eyeliner not brown.

Finally, in 1961, Mattel created what would be their ideal doll. The fifth or #5 Ponytail had a lighter, hollow body and sported a wide variety of hair colors including a vivid red usually called

BLONDE #5 PONYTAIL BARBIE® DOLL IN THEATER DATE, STOCK #959 (US VERSION), CIRCA 1961.
The #5 Ponytail Barbie® doll was the final step in a long process of perfecting the Barbie® doll's image.

BRUNETTE #4 PONYTAIL WITH FACTORY BUN IN ORIGINAL OUTFIT, CIRCA 1960.
This brunette #4 Ponytail came from the factory with upswept hair, rather than the more commonly found Ponytail.
Doll courtesy of Linda Oliva.

"titian." The texture of her hair was different, as well, going from the softer Saran to a harder, more resilient synthetic fiber with harder curly bangs in front. She was also the first doll to wear a foil wrist tag. Her bottom markings now changed to:

Barbie®
Pats. Pending
© MCMLVIII
by
Mattel
Inc.

From time to time, collectors may find vintage dolls that exhibit characteristics of more than one release of doll. These dolls are known as "transitionals" and there is a simple explanation for them. Mattel was producing millions of dolls a year. If extra arms, legs, or heads were produced, it wouldn't have been cost efficient to throw the parts away. So they would continue to be used until every piece was finished up. Therefore, it is not uncommon to find a #3 head on a #4 body or a Ponytail doll with harder curls in the front and softer hair in the back.

TITIAN #5 PONYTAIL BARBIE® DOLL IN SWINGING EASY, STOCK #955, CIRCA 1961.
This is the first issue of the Barbie® doll to have a hair color other than blonde or brunette. Redheaded dolls were made in much smaller numbers, therefore making them more desirable to collectors. This particular doll also has a factory braided ponytail, an unusual hairstyle found on only a few dolls. A blue version of this same outfit was released as Let's Dance, stock #978.

WHITE GINGER BUBBLECUT BARBIE® DOLL IN MOOD FOR MUSIC, STOCK #940, CIRCA 1962.
The hair color on this doll is unusual and not many of them were produced. The Bubblecut doll was also the first doll to be available with a variety of lip colors, not just red.
Doll and outfit courtesy of Linda Oliva.

BLACK BUBBLECUT BARBIE® DOLL IN GOLDEN ELEGANCE, STOCK #992, CIRCA 1961.
Bubblecut Barbie® dolls are probably the most plentiful of all the vintage dolls produced, making them more affordable to collectors.

A second Barbie® doll with a new short bouffant hairdo called the Bubblecut was also released in 1961. The Bubblecut doll proved to be so popular that it was produced until 1966 and is still a favorite with collectors. These dolls are probably the most easily found on the collectors' market,

BLONDE BUBBLECUT BARBIE® DOLL IN ORIGINAL OUTFIT, CIRCA 1963.
The first change to Barbie® doll's hairstyle was this short bouffant style called the Bubblecut. Dolls of this type were available through 1967 and could be found in a variety of hair colors.
Doll courtesy of Linda Oliva.

BRUNETTE #1 (FUZZY HAIR) KEN® DOLL IN SLEEPER SET (BLUE VARIATION), STOCK #0782, CIRCA 1961.
This is the first Ken® doll ever produced by Mattel. The flocked hair is extremely fragile and most dolls of this type are found in various stages of baldness. The Ken® doll was the first companion to be produced for the Barbie® doll, but certainly not the last.

hence their affordability. It is important to note that the 1961 Bubblecut is identical in all ways to the #5 Ponytail except for the hairstyle. This has led some collectors to distinguish those red-lipped, red-nailed dolls as #5 Bubblecuts even though they were the first ones of that type produced.

That same year, Barbie® doll's boyfriend, the Ken® doll also arrived on the scene. Mattel's motivational research had shown that little girls wanted the Barbie® doll to

have a male escort for her adventures. The very first Ken® doll (stock #750, also known as #1 or Fuzzy Headed), was named for the Handlers' son. He stands 12 inches tall, has a six-piece jointed body, painted blue eyes, and a flocked crewcut in either blonde or brown. He wore red bathing trunks and cork sandals, and came with a yellow towel. Because the hair flocking came off in water, resulting in many a prematurely balding Ken® doll, the company re-released him the following year with molded, painted hair instead. The second issue (#2 Ken®) wore red bathing trunks, a red and white candy-striped beach jacket, and cork sandals. He came in either blonde or brunette. His markings read:

> **Ken®**
> **Pat. Pend.**
> **© MCMLX**
> **by**
> **Mattel Inc.**

In 1962, both the Ponytail (also known to collectors as the #6) and Bubblecut Barbie® dolls could be purchased in a variety of hair and lip colors.

Dolls came in assorted shades of blonde, brown, red, and black sporting red, coral, or pink lipstick. Nail color was either red or various shades of coral, which did not necessarily match with the doll's lipstick color. All dolls now wore a new red jersey tank swimsuit, red open-toed mules, pearl stud earrings, and a foil wrist tag. The box art also changed, with a newer, more cartoon style of illustration and pictures of Bubblecut Barbie® dolls modeling newer outfits replacing the older ones.

Based on the popularity of the Bubblecut hairstyle, Mattel decided to release another new doll in 1963; the Fashion Queen Barbie® (stock #870). This doll had molded brown plastic hair and came with three wigs on a white plastic wig-stand (a blonde bubble-on-bubble hairdo, a red flip, and a brunette pageboy) for three totally separate looks. She wore a strapless gold and white striped lamé bathing suit with a matching Egyptian-style turban, faux pearl earrings, and white open-toed shoes. Her lips and nails are in shades of coral or beige and she has a

TITIAN STRAIGHT LEG MIDGE DOLL IN GREEN SILK PAK SHEATH, CIRCA 1963.
This is the first Midge doll ever produced by Mattel. She could wear all of Barbie® doll's clothes and share in her adventures. Midge doll was available as a blonde, brunette, or redhead.

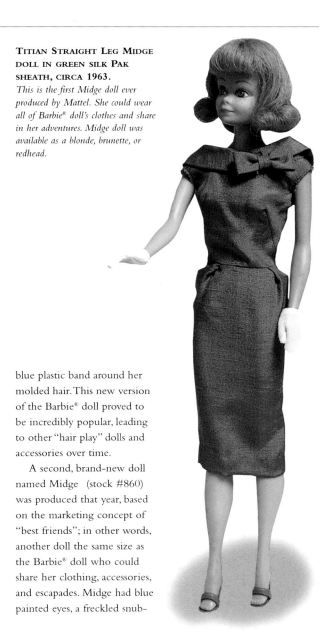

blue plastic band around her molded hair. This new version of the Barbie® doll proved to be incredibly popular, leading to other "hair play" dolls and accessories over time.

A second, brand-new doll named Midge (stock #860) was produced that year, based on the marketing concept of "best friends"; in other words, another doll the same size as the Barbie® doll who could share her clothing, accessories, and escapades. Midge had blue painted eyes, a freckled snub-

nose face, and a perky flip hairstyle. Her two-tone, two-piece jersey bathing suit complemented her variety of hair colors; blue for blonde, red and pink for brunette, and lime and orange for titian. In addition, there are two harder-to-find variations of the straight-legged Midge doll; one has painted teeth, the other lacks freckles.

Both the Fashion Queen Barbie® doll and Midge doll have the same straight-legged body (commonly known as the Midge/Barbie® body) and they share the same markings:

```
         Midge ™
        © 1962
        Barbie®
         © 1958
           by
        Mattel, Inc.
```

A newer version of the Ken® doll was also produced that year. This one is a ¼ inch shorter than the earlier ones, with looser arm and leg joints. The purpose of the new body molding was to make him stand alone more easily. He is identical to earlier editions except that the markings on this Ken® doll read:

FASHION QUEEN BARBIE® DOLL IN BRUNCH TIME, STOCK #1628, CIRCA 1963 AND MOLDED HEAD MIDGE DOLL ON A STRAIGHT-LEGGED BODY IN PAK SHEATH, CIRCA 1965.
Both of these dolls came with sets of three special wigs which could be used to change their looks. Hair play was a big part of 1960s life.

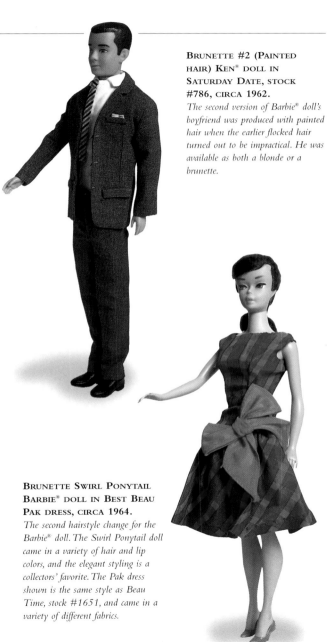

Ken ®
© 1960
by
Mattel, Inc.
Hawthorne
Calif. USA

In 1964, the Barbie® doll underwent yet another hairstyle change. This time, the doll had a sophisticated style consisting of a ponytail with a sleek lock of hair swept across her forehead, known as a Swirl Ponytail to collectors. Hair colors have been found ranging from platinum white (White Ginger) to black, with lipstick colors in white, lavender, pinks, reds, oranges, and corals. The Swirl Ponytail Barbie® doll (stock #0850) had the same Midge/Barbie® body as dolls from the previous year and came in the same red jersey swimsuit.

In addition to the Swirl doll, there was the Miss Barbie® doll (stock #1060). She is the only sleep-eyed doll ever to be produced by Mattel as well as the first Barbie® doll to have bendable rubber legs. She has a molded, hard plastic head, sporting an orange plastic band, and wore a pink

BRUNETTE #2 (PAINTED HAIR) KEN® DOLL IN SATURDAY DATE, STOCK #786, CIRCA 1962.
The second version of Barbie® doll's boyfriend was produced with painted hair when the earlier flocked hair turned out to be impractical. He was available as both a blonde or a brunette.

BRUNETTE SWIRL PONYTAIL BARBIE® DOLL IN BEST BEAU PAK DRESS, CIRCA 1964.
The second hairstyle change for the Barbie® doll. The Swirl Ponytail doll came in a variety of hair and lip colors, and the elegant styling is a collectors' favorite. The Pak dress shown is the same style as Beau Time, stock #1651, and came in a variety of different fabrics.

jersey skirted swimsuit, a fuzzy pink swim cap, and pink open-toed mules. Her three wigs are similar to the Fashion Queen's, but in different colors: a red bubble-on-bubble, a blonde flip, and a brunette pageboy. It is very difficult to find the Miss Barbie® doll in excellent condition due to a chemical reaction between the hard

plastic of her head and the rubber interiors of her wigs and bathing cap. This effectively caused her head to melt, creating grooves and scarring around her face.

Miss Barbie® has the following mark on the back of her neck:

★ © **M.I.** ★

and these marks on her body:

★ © **1958** ★
Mattel, Inc.
U.S. Patented
★ **U.S. Pat. Pend.** ★

WHITE GINGER SWIRL PONYTAIL IN SPORTING CASUALS, STOCK #1648, CIRCA 1964.

MISS BARBIE® DOLL— DREAMLAND, STOCK #1669, CIRCA 1964. *This was the only sleep-eyed doll ever produced by Mattel. She also was the first to have bendable legs, and came with three wigs to change her looks.*

The painted-hair Ken® doll's body was changed again in 1964. This time, his body went back to its original height of the 1962 doll and was also used for his best friend, and Midge doll's boyfriend, Allan (stock #1000). The Allan doll had brown painted eyes, painted, molded auburn hair, and wore blue swimming trunks, a blue, red, and green striped beach jacket, and cork sandals. Both male dolls' body markings read:

★ © 1960 by ★
Mattel Inc.
★ Hawthorne ★
Calif. U.S.A.

BENDABLE LEG MIDGE DOLL IN ABOARD SHIP, STOCK #1631, CIRCA 1965, WITH STRAIGHT LEG ALLAN DOLL IN SAILOR, STOCK #796, CIRCA 1964.

This is the second version of Barbie® doll's best friend, Midge, and the first to have bendable legs. After 1966, the Midge doll would not be seen again for another 25 years. With her is the very first Allan doll, her boyfriend and Ken® doll's best friend.

The other brand-new doll that year was Skipper , Barbie® doll's little sister (stock #0950). She was nine inches tall, with a six-piece, jointed straight-legged body, blue painted eyes, and long silky hair that came in various shades of blonde, brown, or red. She wore a red cotton one-piece sailor suit, red plastic flats, and a brass headband. Her markings read:

Skipper
© 1963
Mattel, Inc.

In 1965, two new friends for Skipper were produced. Skooter (stock #1040) could pass for Midge doll's little sister, while Ricky (stock #1090), a little boy, might be Allan doll's younger brother.

STRAIGHT LEG SKOOTER DOLL IN RED SENSATION, STOCK #1901, CIRCA 1964, RICKY DOLL IN SATURDAY SHOW, STOCK #1502, CIRCA 1964, AND STRAIGHT LEG SKIPPER DOLL IN FUN AT THE FAIR, STOCK #1624, CIRCA 1963.

These are three of the Junior Set dolls: this straight-legged version of Skipper is the very first edition. Skooter was her very first best friend, and Ricky, her first boyfriend.

Skooter wore her red, blonde, or brown hair in two pigtails and came in a two-piece red and white striped swimsuit, while the Ricky doll had brown painted eyes and molded, red painted hair, wearing blue trunks, with matching jacket, and cork sandals. Ricky and Skooter shared the same body as Skipper and their markings read:

© 1963
Mattel Inc.

Like other "best friends" dolls, Skooter could share Skipper doll's wardrobe while Ricky had six outfits of his own.

There are also two types of rarities that have been found which were produced within this time period. The first is

DRESSED BOX DOLLS—#2 KEN® DOLL IN KING ARTHUR, STOCK #0773, BUBBLECUT BARBIE® DOLL IN GUINEVERE, STOCK #0873, CIRCA 1964.
Mattel produced very limited editions of their dolls already dressed in outfits. The boxes varied greatly from the regular issue dolls, with special colored bands and a plastic inner liner with gold seal. Any collection would be enhanced by the addition of any one of these rare items.
Courtesy of Linda Oliva.

31

the "pink silhouette boxed" doll, the other the "dressed boxed" doll. The pink silhouette doll consists of a #1 through #4 Barbie® doll wearing an appropriate tagged Mattel outfit in a specially designed box. The box differs from the standard Barbie® doll box in that it is pink with gray and white silhouettes of the Barbie® doll on the outside. These dolls are believed to have been sold to store owners for store display purposes and are very rare. The box will say "Dressed Display Doll" and usually be marked with the name of the doll and the outfit on the outside of the box, although the stock number may differ from the one normally listed. The second, the dressed box doll, is similar in that it includes a dressed Barbie® doll or Barbie® family doll inside a specially marked box. In the case of the dressed box doll, the box design is closer to the regular edition dolls, but has two colored bands that run along its width. In addition, the dressed box editions have a clear plastic liner with a gold seal which covers the doll and which states the name of the outfit

DRESSED BOX DOLL, BLONDE PONYTAIL BARBIE® DOLL IN ICEBREAKER, STOCK #942, CIRCA 1964.
Courtesy of Linda Oliva.

the doll is wearing. The box lid will say "Dressed Doll" and should have a gold sticker bearing the name of the outfit as well. These specialty dolls were sold as regular store editions from 1964 through 1965 but in much smaller numbers. Both types of dolls are extremely hard to find and quite valuable.

In 1965, the bendable leg Barbie® doll (stock #1070), also known as the American Girl was released. Her new hairstyle was a short, chin-length "Dutch boy" which was available in a variety of colors. Assorted textured fibers were used at different times, so some dolls found have silkier hair, others much coarser. Lip colors also varied, with pinks and corals being the prevalent shades. Unfortunately, many have faded to a sickly butterscotch yellow over time. For the first time, the doll's ears were not pierced and she came wearing a tank swimsuit consisting of a multicolored striped cotton top and turquoise jersey bottom, and matching turquoise open-toed mules. The markings on the doll's buttocks are the same as Miss Barbie® doll's.

A second doll using this body type is the Bendable Leg Midge doll (see page 29). This Midge doll (stock #1080) had a new short bouffant hairdo with bangs, and was available as a blonde, brunette, or redhead. Bendable Leg Midge came wearing a multicolored cotton knit swimsuit and blue mules. In addition, there was a special Midge wig wardrobe set (stock #1009) which featured a hard molded Midge head only (similar to the Fashion Queen head) with orange plastic band and three special wigs: a blonde Swirl n' Curl pageboy, titian Double Ponytail pigtails, and brunette Topknot Pouf.

Several extremely rare editions of the bendable leg Barbie® doll were also released, including those featuring both Swirl Ponytail and Bubblecut heads. However, the most desirable of all American Girl variations is the Side-part Barbie® doll. This doll has full shoulder-length hair styled in a long flip.

SIDE-PART BUBBLECUT BARBIE® DOLL, LEMON BLONDE, 1963.
This is a rare variation of the Bubblecut Barbie® doll. As you can see, she has a very noticeable side part and a side spit curl to differentiate her hairstyle from regular-style Bubblecut dolls.
Courtesy of Linda Oliva.

There is a visible side-part rooted into the hairstyle, and the most common hair color is ash brown. The Side-part doll usually wears a blue satin ribbon headband and the most common lip color is coral.

There were also new Ken®, Allan, Skipper, and Skooter dolls utilizing Mattel's new lifelike bendable leg technology. All dolls had the same markings as previous releases but came in new bathing suits.

The bendable leg dolls continued to be available in 1966. However, some of the later Barbie® dolls have been found with heavier face paint, stronger cheek blush, and lips that ranged from red through raspberry. Most dolls found with this higher color also tend to have longer, shoulder-length hair and are commonly called the Color Magic face since they share the same characteristics of the other Barbie® dolls released that year. These dolls are considered highly collectible. The Color Magic Barbie® doll (stock #1150) featured Mattel's latest innovation: long, straight shoulder-length hair that came in either Golden Blonde or

BLONDE BENDABLE LEG BARBIE® DOLL IN JAPANESE THEATER DATE, CIRCA 1965.
The bendable leg or American Girl Barbie® doll is one of the most popular dolls with collectors. Here is a pristine version modeling the extremely rare Japanese release of Theater Date. American collectors are willing to pay very high prices to obtain foreign variations of American Barbie® doll outfits.
Courtesy of Frank Sposato.

HIGH COLOR BRUNETTE BENDABLE LEG BARBIE® DOLL IN MUSIC CENTER MATINEE, STOCK #1663, CIRCA 1966.
A later version of the American Girl doll, this one has the deeper lip and cheek color known as the "Color Magic" face.

RED BENDABLE LEG BARBIE® DOLL IN GOLD N' GLAMOR, STOCK #1647, CIRCA 1965.
Another example of the American Girl doll. This one wears an outfit from the stock #1600 series, the most popular and most elusive of all regular-issue Barbie® doll outfits. The stock #1600 series of outfits were only produced for one to two years, and usually in very fragile fabrics such as chiffon, making them very difficult to find today.

BRUNETTE BENDABLE LEG BUBBLECUT BARBIE® DOLL, CIRCA 1966.

This is a rare version of the Bendable Leg doll—a Bubblecut head with the high color "Color Magic" face on a Bendable Leg body. Dolls have been found with both the Bubblecut and Swirl Ponytail hairstyles on this type of body, but they are exceedingly rare.

Courtesy of Linda Oliva.

PAK KNIT DRESS AND NRFB MUSIC CENTER MATINEE, STOCK #1663.

Pak outfits like this knit dress were budget mix n' match separates and accessories were sold on these cardboard cards. Regular, more expensive outfits were sold in frame-style boxes with many pieces including small accessories, shoes, and jewelry.

JAPANESE SIDE-PART BARBIE® DOLL IN GALA ABEND, CIRCA 1966.

A second Japanese side-part doll. This one is modeling an exclusive stock #1600 series fashion only available in Europe.

Doll and outfit courtesy of Linda Oliva.

BLONDE BENDABLE LEG KEN® DOLL IN KEN® A GO GO SERIES, STOCK #1423, CIRCA 1965.

The very first issue of the Ken® doll with bendable legs. The outfit he wears is part of the stock #1400 series.

AMERICAN SIDE-PART BARBIE® DOLL IN EVENING GALA, STOCK #1660, CIRCA 1966.
Another rare variation of the Bendable Leg American Girl Barbie® doll. Very few dolls were made with this hairstyle, which accounts for her popularity amongst collectors.
Doll and outfit courtesy of Frank Sposato.

Midnight Black that could be changed to Scarlet Flame or Ruby Red respectively. Her body was the same as Miss Barbie® and American Girl dolls, her legs were bendable, and she came wearing a one-piece diamond-patterned jersey bathing suit and matching headband. The fabric of these, as well as other Color Magic outfits, could also be changed when dipped in the "magic" liquid.

The Barbie® doll's "modern" cousin, Francie , was also made available in 1966. This 11¼-inch teenage doll was given a slimmer, less buxom figure in order to wear all the Mod Carnaby Street-type fashions then in style. The Francie doll came in both a straight-legged version (stock #1140), featuring a blonde or brown flip and brown painted eyes, or a bendable-legged version (stock #1130) with a

BENDABLE LEG ALLAN DOLL IN HIKING HOLIDAY, STOCK #1412, CIRCA 1965.
The second issue, this time produced with bendable legs. Allan was discontinued after 1966 but was brought back as Alan, Midge doll's groom, in a six-doll gift set in 1992.

BENDABLE LEG SKIPPER DOLL IN SCHOOL GIRL, STOCK #1921, BENDABLE LEG SKOOTER DOLL IN SHIP AHOY, STOCK #1918, CIRCA 1965.
Skipper and her best friend joined the bendable leg set in 1965. Like the earlier straight-legged version of these dolls, Skipper and Skooter could share clothing and adventures.

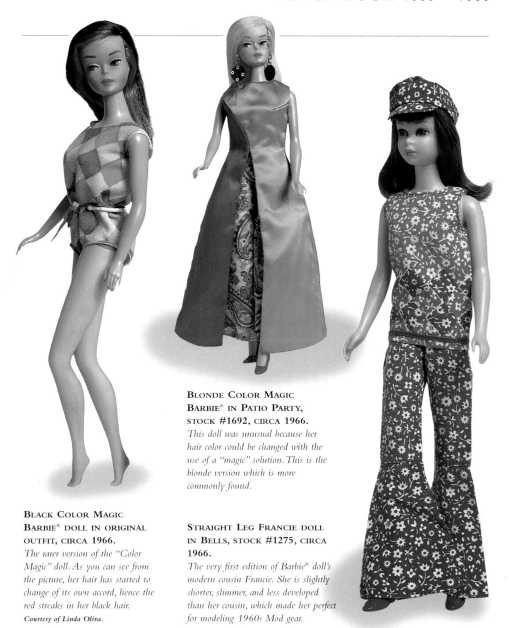

**BLONDE COLOR MAGIC
BARBIE® IN PATIO PARTY,
STOCK #1692, CIRCA 1966.**
*This doll was unusual because her
hair color could be changed with the
use of a "magic" solution. This is the
blonde version which is more
commonly found.*

**BLACK COLOR MAGIC
BARBIE® DOLL IN ORIGINAL
OUTFIT, CIRCA 1966.**
*The rarer version of the "Color
Magic" doll. As you can see from
the picture, her hair has started to
change of its own accord, hence the
red streaks in her black hair.*
Courtesy of Linda Oliva.

**STRAIGHT LEG FRANCIE DOLL
IN BELLS, STOCK #1275, CIRCA
1966.**
*The very first edition of Barbie® doll's
modern cousin Francie. She is slightly
shorter, slimmer, and less developed
than her cousin, which made her perfect
for modeling 1960s Mod gear.*

BRUNETTE AND BLONDE BENDABLE LEG FRANCIE DOLLS IN THE 1966 SEARS' EXCLUSIVE GIFT SET SWINGING SEPARATES, STOCK #1042, CIRCA 1966.

Gift sets like these were available only during the holiday season through mail-order catalogs of selected department stores. They are very rare and very desirable to collectors.

similar hairstyle and eye color but real rooted eyelashes. Straight-legged Francie dolls came in a red and white polka-dot crop top with red and white gingham shorts, while the bendable-legged version came in a one-piece jersey knit bathing suit in either aqua blue or white with a green bottom.

Both Francie dolls' bodies are marked:

> © 1965
> Mattel Inc.
> U.S. Patented
> U.S. Pat. Pend.
> Made in Japan

Two other new dolls, Tutti and Todd , the Barbie® doll's "tiny sister and brother," were also produced in 1966. Tutti (stock #3550) is 6¼ inches tall and has a completely poseable rubber body. She has painted blue eyes, long blonde or brown hair, and came wearing a red checked sunsuit with matching hat. Her marks read:

> © 1965
> Mattel, Inc.
> Japan

ORIGINAL BOX FOR SWINGING SEPARATES GIFT SET, CIRCA 1966.
An example of the box artwork for one of the Sears' Exclusive Gift Sets. Gift set boxes are even rarer than the outfits themselves because they were rarely saved.

brown painted eyes and short red hair. He wore a red, white, and blue plaid cap and shorts with a blue shirt. The only gift set he appears in is *Sundae Treat* (stock #3556) which features both twins (this time Tutti was auburn-haired) in matching red and white striped outfits for an outing in an ice-cream parlor.

Four additional Tutti gift sets were also available: *Walkin' My Dolly*, a sandy blonde-haired Tutti complete with baby doll and carriage (stock #3552); *Night-Night, Sleep-Tight*, a titian Tutti complete with a bedroom set (stock #3553); *Me and My Dog*, a brunette Tutti and her large white furry dog (stock #3554); and *Melody in Pink*, a pale blonde Tutti complete with a piano and piano stool (stock #3555). Another two were released the following year: *Cookin' Goodies*, a black-haired Tutti with a stove and pots and pans (stock #3559) and *Swing-a-ling*, a blonde Tutti featuring a swing set (stock #3560). Todd (stock #3590) was the same size and body type as his twin sister but had

TUTTI AND TODD DOLLS—TUTTI IN COME TO MY PARTY, STOCK #3607, TODD IN ORIGINAL OUTFIT, CIRCA 1966.
Tutti was available as either a single doll or in a series of special gift sets and had her own line of clothing. Todd was available on his own or with Tutti in a gift set called Sundae Treat. He had no separate clothes of his own in the United States, although in Europe quite a number were produced.

THE MOD ERA
1967 – 1972

In 1967, the Barbie® doll was given a total transformation as she went as Mod as her cousin Francie. Sporting a newly sculpted face with a more youthful look, both the new Standard Barbie® doll (stock #1190) and Twist 'n Turn™ Barbie® doll (stock #1160) had long, straight hair in Summer Sand, Chocolate Bon Bon, Go Go Co Co, and Sun Kissed. The Standard Barbie® doll had a straight-legged body identical to that of the earlier dolls, as well as painted eyelids. Her body markings read:

> **Midge™**
> © 1962
> **Barbie®**
> © 1958
> **by Mattel**

The Standard Barbie® doll's skin tone was generally much pinker than that of the earlier dolls but, occasionally, dolls have been found with the older, grayer bodies. She originally wore a hot pink

BLONDE TWIST 'N TURN™ BARBIE® DOLL IN ZOKKO, STOCK #1820, CIRCA 1967. *This Barbie® doll heralded the Mod era with her new face mold, rooted eyelashes, Twist 'n Turn™ waist, and bendable legs. As newer, younger collectors are becoming aware of vintage dolls, the Twist 'n Turn™ and other Mod era dolls are becoming more and more popular.*

bikini with a white plastic flower sewn on the hip.

The Twist 'n Turn™ Barbie® doll (stock #1160) not only had rooted eyelashes and bendable legs, but a waist that swiveled back and forth, allowing all sorts of new posing possibilities. She came wearing an orange vinyl bikini, under a white fishnet mesh cover-up, and had the following marks on her bottom:

> ©1966
> Mattel Inc.
> U.S. Patented
> U.S. Pat. Pend.
> Made In
> Japan

Unfortunately, the "©1966" tends to create confusion with collectors since many dolls have been found with that mark. The Twist 'n Turn™ waist mechanism was patented that year, and is still being used on most Barbie® dolls currently in production today. However Mattel has changed its production sites more than once since then, so only Twist 'n Turn™ dolls made in Japan or Taiwan are actually from this time period.

BRUNETTE TWIST 'N TURN™ IN SEARS' EXCLUSIVE OUTFIT GLIMMER GLAMOR, STOCK #1547 (1968), CIRCA 1967.
Another view of the first Twist 'n Turn™ Barbie® doll. The outfit she wears was only available through Sears Roebuck stores for one season and is extremely difficult to find, partially due to the fragile materials it's made of.
Doll and outfit courtesy of Linda Oliva.

BROWNETTE STANDARD BARBIE® DOLL IN SEARS' EXCLUSIVE BEAUTIFUL BLUES GIFT SET, STOCK #3303, CIRCA 1967.
The Standard doll was similar to the Twist 'n Turn™ but had a straight-legged, straight-waisted body and painted eyelashes.
Doll and outfit courtesy of Linda Oliva.

Twist 'n Turn™ Francie (stock #1170) was also available that year as either a blonde or brunette, also sporting rooted eyelashes. She comes wearing a one-piece swimsuit with a multicolored striped top and pink vinyl bottom. A second Twist 'n Turn™ Francie doll called Colored Francie (stock #1100) was also issued. This brown-haired, brown-eyed African-American doll is quite beautiful, but extremely rare since she did not sell well at the time. This is probably because she was marketed as Barbie® doll's cousin, rather than a friend of Francie doll's!

#1 COLORED FRANCIE DOLL IN MIDI BOUQUET, STOCK #3446, CIRCA 1967.
This is the first edition of the rare Colored Francie doll which can be distinguished from the later version by her oxidized hair and lighter eye color. This doll did not sell well when first produced but is now one of the most sought-after vintage collectible dolls around.

BRUNETTE TWIST 'N TURN™ FRANCIE IN QUICK SHIFT, STOCK #1266, CIRCA 1967.
This is the first Twist 'n Turn™ Francie doll produced. Like her cousin, Barbie® doll, she has rooted eyelashes, a Twist 'n Turn™ waist and bendable legs.

Colored Francie (also known as Black Francie by collectors) comes dressed in a psychedelic patterned two-piece bathing suit with a sheer chiffon overlay. This issue of the doll will often have reddish hair, due to oxidization of the hair fibers, and light brown or rust colored eyes. Both dolls have the same body markings as the Twist 'n Turn™ Barbie®, despite the difference in body size.

The same is true for the Twist 'n Turn™ Casey doll (stock #1180) Francie doll's hip friend, and the Francie-sized Twiggy doll (stock #1185), the first celebrity doll issued by Mattel. Casey wears her blonde or brown hair in a geometric bob and comes in a white and gold lamé swimsuit with a single dangle earring, while Twiggy, based on "London's Top Teen Model" was blonde, wearing a yellow, blue, and green striped cotton mini dress, yellow panties, and yellow rubber go-go boots. Both dolls have rooted eyelashes and the identical body to Francie.

The last new doll for 1967 was Tutti doll's best friend Chris (stock #3570). Chris could be found with either

BLONDE TWIST 'N TURN™ CASEY DOLL IN PINK LIGHTNING, STOCK #1231, CIRCA 1967.
This is one of Francie doll's two friends produced by Mattel and the epitome of Mod fashion.

BRUNETTE TWIST 'N TURN™ CASEY DOLL IN SEARS' EXCLUSIVE GIFT SET CASEY GOES CASUAL, STOCK #3304, CIRCA 1967.
This gift set is the only time Casey ever had any clothing made especially for her. A separate jumpsuit and vinyl coat were also part of this gift set.

**TWIGGY DOLL IN
TWIGGY GEAR,
STOCK #1728,
CIRCA 1967.**
*The Twiggy doll was
based on the top teen
fashion model in
swinging London
during this time
period. She was made
from the Casey doll
mold and only
available as a blonde.
In 1996, the real
Twiggy starred in an
infomercial for the My
Fair Lady Barbie® doll
series.*

**IN PRINTS, STOCK #1288 NRFB, TWIGGY
TURNOUTS, STOCK #1726 NRFB.**
*Two Francie-size Mod era fashions. There were four outfits
made exclusively for Twiggy.*

BRUNETTE CHRIS, BLONDE CHRIS, AND CARLA MODEL DIFFERENT PIECES OF THE 1967 FUNTIMERS GIFT SET.
Chris was available as both a blonde and brunette. The Carla doll was only available in Europe in the 1970s.

BOX ART FOR SEARS' EXCLUSIVE CHRIS FUNTIMERS, STOCK #3301, CIRCA 1967.
This is the only time Tutti doll's friend Chris had her own outfits.

BRUNETTE TALKING BARBIE® IN 1969 JC PENNEY EXCLUSIVE PINK PREMIÈRE, STOCK #1596, CIRCA 1968.
The very first Talking Barbie® doll. She said six separate phrases when her string was pulled. She has rooted eyelashes and bendable legs.
Outfit courtesy of Linda Oliva.

BLONDE TALKING BARBIE® IN SEARS EXCLUSIVE GOLDEN GROOVE, STOCK #1593, CIRCA 1968.
This is another example of the first Talking Barbie® doll. Unfortunately, these dolls were made with a design flaw which leaves their hip joints very weak. Many times, these talkers will be found with one or both legs broken off, even if never removed from the box. Luckily, they can be repaired by a reputable doll restorer.
Doll and outfit courtesy of Linda Oliva.

blonde or brunette hair, brown painted eyes, and a psychedelic print mini dress with matching panties.

In 1968, the Mod trend continued as Mattel released their first talking doll, the Talking Barbie® (stock #1115). She could be made to say one

of six phrases by pulling a string on the base of the doll's neck attached to an internal record player. Talking Barbie® used the same face mold as the Twist 'n Turn™ doll and also had rooted eyelashes and bendable legs. However, her hands were different. Barbie®

dolls made in Japan all had separated fingers while dolls made in Mexico had slender hands with fingers undivided.

Like the Twist 'n Turn™ doll, Talking Barbie® was available in the same four hair colors. Her hair was styled in a side ponytail with three hot pink bows and spit curls. She came wearing a hot pink woven top with matching vinyl shorts. Her markings read:

© 1967
Mattel Inc.
U.S. & Foreign
Pats. Pend.
Mexico

Barbie® doll's two new friends, the Talking Stacey (stock #1125) and Talking Christie (stock #1126) dolls were also premièred this year. Stacey, a swinging Londoner with a British accent, had a long side ponytail in a choice of blonde or red hair, while Christie, Barbie® doll's first African-American friend, wore a dark brown modified Afro hairstyle.

Both had the same body type as the Talking Barbie® doll with identical markings. However, each said six different phrases. In addition to the American edition, Mattel also made a rarer Spanish Talker (stock #8348). The Spanish doll was identical to the American except that she spoke Spanish and had the Japanese-style hands.

BLONDE TALKING STACEY IN EXTRAVAGANZA, STOCK #1844, CIRCA 1968.
Barbie® doll's friend Stacey also said six different things. During the Mod era, London was the fashion center of the world so, of course, a trendy, modern girl like Barbie® doll would have a British chum like Stacey.

TALKING CHRISTIE, CIRCA 1968, AND TALKING BRAD , IN ORIGINAL OUTFITS, CIRCA 1970.
Mattel was one of the first toy companies to mass produce African-American dolls during the 1960s. What makes Christie and Brad even more unique is that they were made from new molds rather than just black versions of existing white dolls.

A Twist 'n Turn™ version of Stacey (stock #1165) was also available with the same body markings as Twist 'n Turn™ Barbie®, as well as a new Twist 'n Turn™ Skipper (stock #1105) doll. Stacey had a long ponytail in either red or blonde, while Skipper had long straight hair and was available in a variety of colors. The Skipper doll's body markings read:

© 1967 Mattel Inc.
★ U.S. Pat'd ★
U.S. Pats. Pend
★ Made in Japan ★

Later editions of the Twist 'n Turn™ Skipper may be marked "Made in Taiwan."

A second issue of the Twist 'n Turn™ Colored Francie doll was also released—this time the doll had darker painted eyes and hair made out of a new fiber which retains its color. All the Talking dolls as well as the Twist 'n Turn™ dolls had rooted eyelashes.

Tutti gained a new famous friend in 1968—Buffy , based on Anissa Jones' character from the popular comedy *Family Affair*. She had blonde hair tied in pigtails, a red and white

BLONDE TWIST 'N TURN™ STACEY IN SEARS EXCLUSIVE STRIPES ARE HAPPENING, STOCK #1545, CIRCA 1968.
This is the first Twist 'n Turn™ edition of Stacey, as well as the first of two gift sets to bear her name. Like previous Twist 'n Turn™ dolls, she has rooted eyelashes, a Twist 'n Turn™ waist, and bendable legs.

BRUNETTE TWIST 'N TURN™ SKIPPER IN POPOVER, STOCK #1943, CIRCA 1968.
The Skipper doll went Mod for the first time and was available with a Twist 'n Turn™ waist, rooted eyelashes, and a variety of hair colors.

polka-dot dress, and red panties. In her arms, she carried her trademark rag doll, Mrs. Beasley.

Spurred on by the success of both the Twiggy and Buffy dolls, Mattel created their next two celebrity dolls in 1969. Julia , based on Diahann Carroll's popular television nurse character, was adapted from the Christie head mold and was available as both a Talking and Twist 'n Turn™ doll. Twist 'n Turn™ Julia (stock #1127) wore a nurse's uniform and cap. The first edition of the uniform was a two-piece skirt and blouse; the later, more common issue was a one-piece dress. Talking Julia (stock #1128) came wearing a gold and silver Lurex™ jumpsuit. Earlier issues had short straight hair; later ones an Afro hairdo. Both dolls had the same markings as previous Twist 'n Turn™ and Talking dolls. Like the earlier version of Colored Francie, the fiber in early Julia dolls tends to oxidize, causing their hair color to change into a variety of shades from burgundy through bright rust red.

Barbie® doll's other celebrity friend, Truly Scrumptious , was

TWIST 'N TURN™ JULIA DOLL, CIRCA 1969.
This was the first African-American celebrity doll produced by Mattel from the Christie mold and based on the TV nurse and single parent played by Diahann Carroll.

THE #2 BLACK FRANCIE DOLL IN 1968 SEARS EXCLUSIVE OUTFIT ORANGE ZIP (NO STOCK NUMBER), CIRCA 1968.
The second version of the "Colored" Francie has black hair and darker eyes. She's wearing a rare outfit that was produced only for Sears Roebuck for the 1968 holiday season.

TALKING TRULY SCRUMPTIOUS AND STANDARD TRULY SCRUMPTIOUS DOLLS, CIRCA 1969.
Both versions of the doll were based on the fabulous leading lady of the children's film Chitty Chitty Bang Bang *played by Sally Ann Howes.*

based on the *Chitty Chitty Bang Bang* film character as played by Sally Ann Howes, and was available in either a Standard (stock #1107) or Talking (stock #1108) edition. Truly was adapted from the Francie mold. She has straight blonde hair, pulled off her face, blue eyes, and rooted eyelashes. The Standard doll came wearing a pale pink and white costume while the Talking doll's outfit was magenta and black. Both of these Truly Scrumptious dolls are extremely difficult to find and are very collectible, with the Standard being the more commonly available of the two. The Standard doll has the same markings as previous Standard Barbie® dolls while the Talking Truly Scrumptious doll is marked as:

> ★ © 1967 ★
> Mattel Inc.
> U.S. & Foreign
> Pats. Pend.
> ★ Mexico ★

Another friend produced in 1969 was the New n' Groovy Talking PJ doll (stock #1113). PJ was made from the now discontinued Midge mold and wore a pink and orange floral print tricot mini dress with matching pink "bloomers." Her straight blonde hair was styled in two pigtails wrapped with love beads, and she had rooted eyelashes. Like other Talking dolls, her marks read:

> Talking PJ
> © 1967
> Mattel Inc
> U.S. & Foreign
> Pats. Pend.
> Mexico

The Ken® doll, like Midge, had been gone from the scene for over a year. The new Talking Ken® doll (stock #1111) arrived in 1969. He said six different phrases, sported a more mature-looking head mold with molded brown painted hair, a more muscular body, and bendable legs. The marks on his buttocks are:

> © 1968
> Mattel Inc
> U.S. & For. Pat'd
> Other Pat's
> Pending
> Mexico

Several dolls previously in production underwent

TWIST 'N TURN™ PJ IN SEARS SWINGING IN SILVER GIFT SET, STOCK #1588, CIRCA 1970.
Barbie® doll's "new and groovy" friend PJ in the one gift set outfit created exclusively for her. The Talking PJ doll, which was produced a year earlier, was identical to this Twist 'n Turn™ version.
Doll and outfit courtesy of Linda Oliva.

BROWNETTE TALKING BARBIE® AND TALKING KEN®— SEARS EXCLUSIVE FABULOUS FORMAL GIFT SET, STOCK #1595, CIRCA 1968 AND 1969.
The first appearance of the new and improved Ken® doll mold as a Talking Ken® doll. Not only did he have an entirely new face, but his body was more muscular too. This is the Sears gift set featuring both the dolls together, plus the two outfits they're wearing. The Barbie® doll's dress is a variation on her pink Romantic Ruffles ensemble, stock #1871, while the Ken® doll is a variation of Guruvy Formal, stock #1431, which had a red jacket instead.
Barbie® doll and outfits courtesy of Linda Oliva.

makeovers that year. The Twist 'n Turn™ Barbie® doll (stock #1160) changed her hairstyle to a fashionably long flip hairdo with a spit curl in front, and was available in blonde, light brown, and darker brunette. Twist 'n Turn™ Stacey (stock #1165) also went much shorter with a tightly rolled side-part pageboy in either red or blonde. Twist 'n Turn™ Francie (stock #1170) changed her hair to a short tightly curled style with a matching headband, while the Twist 'n Turn™ Skipper doll (stock #1105) now sported two sausage-curl pigtails and bangs. Each doll was also released in a newly designed bathing suit, but their body markings remain the same.

BRUNETTE TWIST 'N TURN™ BARBIE® IN DANCING LIGHTS, STOCK #3437, CIRCA 1969.
This is the later version of the Twist 'n Turn™ Barbie® with her new Marlo Thomas-inspired flip hairdo.

BLONDE TWIST 'N TURN™ BARBIE® IN MINI PRINTS, STOCK #1809, CIRCA 1969.
Like the early Twist 'n Turn™ Barbie®, this doll has rooted eyelashes, bendable legs, and a moveable waist.

BLONDE AND BRUNETTE TWIST 'N TURN™ FRANCIE DOLLS IN JC PENNEY EXCLUSIVE SPORTING SET GIFT SET, STOCK #1044, CIRCA 1969.

Two Francie dolls showing off their new look, as well as the very elusive gift set outfits they're wearing.

Dolls and outfits courtesy of Linda Oliva.

RED TWIST 'N TURN™ STACEY DOLL IN MAXI 'N MINI, STOCK #1799, CIRCA 1969.

This is the later version of Twist 'n Turn™ Stacey sporting her new hairstyle. Like many other ensembles of this time period, this outfit is difficult to find in good condition because of the fragile fabrics involved.

BRUNETTE TALKING BARBIE® IN PARTY LINES (VARIATION), STOCK #3490, CIRCA 1970.
This later version of the Talking Barbie® has both a different hairstyle and a different set of phrases that she says. The dress she's wearing is a rare variation of Party Lines which is usually found made out of black satin with a pink floral design.

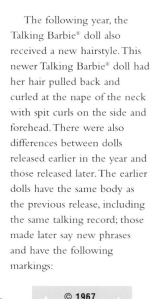

The following year, the Talking Barbie® doll also received a new hairstyle. This newer Talking Barbie® doll had her hair pulled back and curled at the nape of the neck with spit curls on the side and forehead. There were also differences between dolls released earlier in the year and those released later. The earlier dolls have the same body as the previous release, including the same talking record; those made later say new phrases and have the following markings:

> ★ © 1967 ★
> Mattel Inc.
> U.S. & Foreign
> Pats. Pend.
> ★ Hong Kong ★

REDHAIRED TALKING BARBIE® IN ORIGINAL OUTFIT, CIRCA 1970.
Another view of the later version of Talking Barbie®.

TWIST 'N TURN™ CHRISTIE IN SPECIAL SPARKLE, STOCK #1468, CIRCA 1970.
Like many other African-American dolls of this time period, this Twist 'n Turn™ Christie has oxidized hair.

Two extremely rare versions of the Talking Barbie® doll were also produced. One is American, the other is Spanish-speaking. The big difference is that their heads were produced from the Stacey mold rather than the Standard Barbie® doll mold. The American doll was made in Mexico, the Spanish-speaking model was manufactured in Hong Kong.

In addition, both Christie (stock #1119) and PJ (stock #1118) were produced with the Twist 'n Turn™ body as in 1970. The head molds on both dolls were identical to their talking counterparts and the body markings the same as the Twist 'n Turn™ Barbie® doll.

That same year, Mattel also produced their most poseable lifelike doll to date—the Dramatic New Living Barbie®. Unlike dolls of the past, this Barbie® doll was so well articulated that not only could she bend her legs and twist her waist but her arms bent at the wrists and elbows, her ankles bent (allowing her to wear both flat and high heeled shoes), her head moved in all directions, and her arm and leg sockets rotated enough to

BLONDE TWIST 'N TURN™ SKIPPER IN BUDDING BEAUTY, STOCK #1731, CIRCA 1969.
This is the later edition of the Twist 'n Turn™ Skipper doll. Like the earlier doll, she has bendable legs, a Twist 'n Turn™ waist, and rooted eyelashes, and was available in a number of hair colors.

LIVING BARBIE® IN FESTIVAL FASHION, STOCK #1056, CIRCA 1970.
Unlike Mattel's other dolls, this Barbie® doll could be posed in any number of ways thanks to her bendable elbows, knees, wrists, ankles, and waist, plus more flexible arm and leg joints.

let her do previously impossible actions such as sitting on horseback, doing gymnastics, or ballet dancing. Living Barbie® had straight shoulder-length hair with thick bangs and was available in platinum blonde, dark brunette, and titian. She had rooted eyelashes and incredibly beautiful face paint. Her lips are usually a shade of orange red. Her markings read:

© 1968 Mattel Inc.
U.S. & For. Pat'd
Other Pats Pend.
★ Taiwan ★

There was also an identical doll *made in Japan* for the Sears' Action Accents gift set. That doll's markings will indicate this on the bottom line. Living Barbie® came in a one-piece bathing suit, half gold, half silver lamé, and a dark coral hooded jacket with gold trim.

A new Living Skipper (stock #1115) was also produced that year. Like her older sister, this Skipper doll could be posed in a variety of ways. Living Skipper wore her hair in two curly pigtails, with a spit curl on her forehead, and had very vivid

LIVING SKIPPER IN SWEET ORANGE, STOCK #3465, CIRCA 1970 AND LIVING FLUFF IN 1974 SEARS EXCLUSIVE SEPARATES, CIRCA 1971.
Skipper and her new friend Fluff were nearly as poseable as the Living Barbie® doll. Both of these dolls were only available as blondes.

face paint, painted blue eyes, and rooted eyelashes. Her hair was only available in blonde, although there is some variation in the shades of the fibers. Her tricot bathing suit was pink, blue, and green, and her body marks read:

© 1969 Mattel Inc
★ Taiwan ★
U.S. & For. Pat'd.
★ Other Pats. Pend. ★
Pat'd. in Canada in 1967

Barbie® doll also gained a new friend in 1970. Walking Jamie (stock #1132) was made from the Barbie® doll head mold as a Sears exclusive. She had brown eyes, rooted lashes and was available as either a blonde, brunette, or redhead. She was the first doll in the Barbie® doll family to walk; a special button on her back made her arms, head, and legs move in a walking motion. Walking Jamie came in a yellow knit mini dress, with orange go-go boots, and was marked as follows:

© 1967 Mattel Inc.
★ U.S. Patented ★
Pat'd Canada 1967
Other Pats. Pend.
★ Japan ★

That same year, another new friend and Christie's boyfriend, the Brad doll, was produced. Brad was the first male African-American doll ever produced by Mattel and was the same size as the Ken® doll. He has brown painted eyes, and black painted hair styled in a short Afro hairstyle, and came wearing an African print dashiki-style shirt with matching swim trunks. There were two different versions of the Brad doll. The first, the Talking Brad (stock #1114) was marked:

© 1968
Mattel Inc.
U.S. & For. Pat'd
Other Pats.
Pending
Mexico

The second, Bendable Leg Brad (stock #1142) shares markings with the new Bendable Leg Ken® (stock #1124) which was released the same year:

BENDABLE LEG BRAD IN BOLD GOLD, STOCK #1436, CIRCA 1970.
The second version of Brad had bendable legs. Later editions were produced of a darker vinyl than earlier ones, giving him a more ethnic look.

SEARS EXCLUSIVE WALKING JAMIE DOLL, NEVER REMOVED FROM THE BOX, CIRCA 1970.
Barbie® doll's newest friend made from the Barbie® doll mold.

PRETTY PAIRS LORI N' RORI, ANGIE N' TANGIE, AND NAN N' FRAN, CIRCA 1970, AND BUFFY AND MRS. BEASLEY, CIRCA 1968.

© 1968
Mattel Inc
US & For. Pat'd
Other Pat's
Pending
Mexico

Later editions of both versions of Brad as well as the Bendable Leg Ken® were produced in Hong Kong and the marks changed accordingly.

Tutti also gained a group of new friends in 1970. The Pretty Pairs sets consisted of a doll sharing the same body as Tutti, and her companion toy, similar in design to the earlier Buffy and Mrs. Beasley. The three Pretty Pairs are:

★ Lori n' Rori (stock #1133), a blonde girl in a blue and white cotton party dress with a brown velour teddy bear.

HAIR HAPPENIN'S FRANCIE IN SNAZZ, STOCK #1225, CIRCA 1970.

The first Francie doll that was only available as a blonde. This doll had a Twist 'n Turn™ body and came with additional hairpieces so that her look could be changed.

★ Nan n' Fran (stock #1134), an African-American girl in a brushed cotton white floral nightie, and matching nightcap, with an African-American baby doll dressed in a pink sleeper suit.

★ Angie n' Tangie (stock #1135), a brunette girl in an orange cotton, lace-trimmed party dress with a rag doll with yellow yarn hair and a matching dress.

In addition to all these new dolls, 1970 also saw newer editions of previous Mattel releases. Two new editions of the Francie doll were produced that year, both only available in blonde. The first was Hair Happenin's Francie (stock #1122). She came in a blue tricot mini dress with lace trim and wore her hair in a short pageboy with bangs. However, her look could be changed over and over again with the addition of four hairpieces included in the set. Hair Happenin's Francie had rooted eyelashes and a Twist 'n Turn™ body with the following markings:

© 1966
Mattel Inc
U.S. Patented
U.S. Pat. Pend.
Made In
Japan

FRANCIE WITH GROWIN' PRETTY HAIR IN SWEET N' SWINGING, STOCK #1288, CIRCA 1970.
This is another edition of the Francie doll centered around a hair play concept. Her long ponytail could be shortened or lengthened by tugging on it. She was only available as a blonde.

The concept of the second doll, Francie With Growin' Pretty Hair (stock #1129), also incorporated hair play. However, this doll had a new hollow body which contained a "Growin' Pretty hairpiece," which could be shortened or lengthened by pulling it on the top of her head. Francie With Growin' Pretty Hair also had bendable legs, rooted eyelashes, and pale blonde hair pulled into an upsweep in order to hide the hole in the crown of her head needed to

contain the hairpiece. Unfortunately, the elastic cord holding the hairpiece inside the Growin' Pretty mechanism often deteriorates and breaks, leaving the rest of the doll intact. This doll is marked:

© 1966
Mattel Inc
U.S. Pat. Other
Pats. Pend
Pat. Canada
1967
Japan

The dolls produced in 1971 continued in the same vein as those the previous year. However, Mattel began to market their dolls in a new way. Rather than making one basic doll with a choice of hair color or style and many different outfits, they produced a variety of different dolls and many fewer outfits. In addition, the only shade of hair to be found was blonde.

Like Dramatic New Living Barbie®, Live Action Barbie® (stock #1152) was fully

LIVE ACTION CHRISTIE, KEN®, BARBIE®, AND PJ, CIRCA 1971.
*The Woodstock era finally hits Barbie® doll and her friends, with new bodies that allow them to
be more poseable than ever.*

poseable. However, this time her waist joint was even looser so that she could dance when rocked back and forth on her special stand. Live Action Barbie® came in blonde only. She had real rooted eyelashes. Her hair was straight, long, and center parted, held in place with a fake suede headband. She wore a two-piece tie-dyed, bell-bottom pants suit with fringed fake suede accessories.

Along with the Barbie® doll, there was also a Live Action Christie (stock #1175) with long, straight black hair, dressed in a purple psychedelic print pants suit and Live Action PJ (stock #1156) with shoulder-length, center-parted blonde hair in an orange mini dress and purple fake suede fringed vest. All three female Live Action dolls had identical bodies and their markings read:

© 1968
Mattel Inc.
U.S. & Foreign Patented
Patented in Canada 1967
Other Patents Pending
Taiwan

There was also a Live Action Ken® (stock #1159) to match the set. This Ken® doll had painted, molded brown hair, gold satin pants, psychedelic print shirt, and a fringed vest. His markings read:

> © 1968
> Mattel Inc
> Taiwan
> U.S. & For. Pat'd
> Patented In
> Canada 1967
> Other Pats.
> Pending

Live Action Barbie®, Ken®, and PJ were also available in separate "On Stage" gift sets that included an extra seven-inch 45rpm record, a battery-operated motorized stage, and plastic microphone and instruments.

Another new friend with the Living Body was Skipper doll's friend Living Fluff (stock #1143). Fluff had blonde hair with bangs styled in two pigtails and came wearing a yellow, orange, and green playsuit. She also had her own yellow skateboard to prove she was always on the go. Her body was identical to that of the Living Skipper doll and had the same body markings.

The next doll released in 1971 was Barbie® with Growin' Pretty Hair (stock #1144). Like the previous year's Francie with Growin'

Pretty Hair, she had a special long ponytail which could be lengthened or shortened by just tugging on it. She also had two extra hairpieces, flowers, ribbons, and other accessories. Like the Live Action Barbie®, she was only available as a blonde. She had real rooted eyelashes and her eyes were centered, not side glancing. She came in a pink satin gown, with attached pink tricot panties, and pink shoes. Her markings read:

> © 1967
> Mattel Inc.
> U.S. Patented
> Other Patents Pending
> Patented in Canada 1967
> Taiwan

In 1972, an identical doll was released in a red, white, and blue granny gown and a slightly modified hairstyle.

In addition, Barbie® Hair Happenin's (stock #1174) was released in 1971. This doll was a department store exclusive and one of the last redheaded Barbie® dolls to be produced for the next 20 years. She wore her hair in a short, center-parted style, and came with three titian hairpieces to

HAIR HAPPENIN'S BARBIE® IN MOVIE GROOVIE, STOCK #1866 AND LAMB N' LEATHER, STOCK #1467, CIRCA 1971.
This department-store exclusive came with hairpieces that allowed her to change her look. She was one of the last dolls to be produced as a redhead for close to 20 years.

change her stylish look. She has the newer centered eyes, with rooted eyelashes, while her dress was pink and white tricot with attached panties and a black velveteen belt. Her body is the Twist 'n Turn™ type and the markings on the doll are identical to those produced earlier.

That same year, new Talking, Twist 'n Turn™, Standard and Living Barbie® dolls were still available. These dolls were all identical to prior releases except that they wore new swimsuits and had the new centered eyes. Several dolls also underwent changes in hairstyling that year. The Twist 'n Turn™ Francie doll (stock #1170) was given a new teased flip hairdo, which is commonly known to collectors as the "No Bangs" look, while Christie and Julia were given the then trendier Afro styles. Otherwise, these dolls remained identical to previous issues.

BARBIE® WITH GROWIN' PRETTY HAIR IN RED WHITE AND WARM, STOCK #1491, CIRCA 1971.
Like the earlier Francie doll with the similar name, this doll's hairstyle could be changed by tugging on her ponytail. She was only available as a blonde.

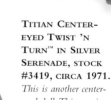

TITIAN CENTER-EYED TWIST 'N TURN™ IN SILVER SERENADE, STOCK #3419, CIRCA 1971.
This is another center-eyed doll. This one is a rare titian-haired doll in the equally rare Silver Serenade outfit.
Doll and outfit courtesy of Linda Oliva.

BROWNETTE CENTER-EYED STANDARD BARBIE® DOLL IN SEARS EXCLUSIVE VELVETEENS, STOCK #1818, CIRCA 1971.
The last variation on the Mod face featured eyes that were centered instead of side glancing.
Doll and outfit courtesy of Linda Oliva.

Also new in 1971 was the first of the Malibu series dolls. Obviously intended as a budget line, these dolls came with no frills in relatively plain packaging. Malibu Barbie® (stock #1067), Malibu Francie (stock #1068), Malibu Skipper (stock #1069), and Malibu Ken® (stock #1088) were the first dolls to have suntanned skin, straight blonde hair, and painted eyelashes. Their bodies were the Twist 'n Turn™ type with identical markings and all came in simple tricot bathing suits with a matching terry cloth towel and plastic sunglasses. Malibu PJ (stock #1187) joined the group in 1972 with Malibu Christie (stock #7745) in 1973. This line has proven so successful that Mattel has continued to release a similar group of dolls every year.

In 1972 Mattel released the inventive Walk Lively series of dolls, who, like the previous Walking Jamie, could walk by themselves. They also brought out the Busy series who could hold things in their hands and the Busy Talking series, the talking version of the Busy dolls.

TWIST 'N TURN™ FRANCIE IN OLDE LOOK, STOCK #3458, CIRCA 1971.
She is the last version of the Twist 'n Turn™ Francie to be produced, commonly known to collectors as the "No Bangs" Francie.

MALIBU BARBIE®, IN ORIGINAL OUTFIT, CIRCA 1971.
The first Malibu Barbie® doll, and the first in a continuing line of budget bathing-suit dolls.

Walk Lively Barbie® (stock #1182), Walk Lively Steffie (stock #1183), Walk Lively Ken® (stock #1184), and Walk Lively Miss America (stock #3200) came with special Walk n' Turn stands which allowed them to move their head and limbs when pushed. Walk Lively Barbie® had long, blonde, center-parted hair, while her new friend Steffie had brown painted eyes and long brunette hair worn in a long flip. Miss America, also made from the Steffie mold, had blue eyes and shorter, curlier brunette hair. All three dolls had rooted eyelashes and bendable legs. All of their bodies are marked:

WALK LIVELY STEFFIE IN INTRIGUE, STOCK #1470, CIRCA 1972.
The Steffie head mold is one of the most popular with collectors and was used on many dolls through the early 1990s.

WALK LIVELY BARBIE® IN FIRELIGHTS, STOCK #1481, CIRCA 1972.

© 1967
Mattel Inc
U.S. Pat. Pend.
Taiwan

Walk Lively Ken® had the same head mold as previous Mod Ken® releases and his body markings read:

© 1968 Mattel Inc
U.S. Pat. Pend
Taiwan

WALK LIVELY MISS AMERICA, CIRCA 1972.
This is another doll made from the Steffie mold.

Busy Barbie® (stock #3311), Busy Steffie (stock #3312), Busy Francie (stock #3313), and Busy Ken® (stock #3314) all had bendable wrists, arms, and legs as well as specially constructed plastic hands which enabled them to hold a variety of accessories. The thumb on each hand is articulated and will open and close by bending the wrist. In addition, they all have bendable wrists, elbows, and knees. Busy Barbie® had long, straight blonde hair held by a brass barrette, centered eyes, and painted eyelashes. Busy Steffie has long brown hair and blue painted eyes, while Francie has a blonde shag hairstyle and brown painted eyes. Busy Ken® looks the same as previous Mod Ken® dolls.

Busy Barbie® and Steffie doll's body marks read:

© 1966
Mattel Inc.
U.S. & Foreign
Patented
Other Pat's
Pending
Made in
U.S.A.

BUSY BARBIE® IN BEST BUY, STOCK #8688, CIRCA 1972.
This doll has unique "busy" hands which can hold a number of accessories. She has bendable legs and elbows and painted lashes.

BUSY FRANCIE IN RIGHT FOR STRIPES, STOCK #3367, CIRCA 1972.
She was one of the last Francie dolls to be produced, and the only one to have "busy" hands.

Francie is marked:

© 1966
Mattel Inc
Hong Kong
U.S. & Foreign
Patented
Other Pat's
Pending

BUSY STEFFIE IN OH BOY CORDUROY, STOCK #3486, CIRCA 1972.
Another Busy Hands doll, this one made from the Steffie mold, has the same characteristics as the Barbie® doll of the same name.

Busy Ken® is marked:

© 1968
Mattel Inc
Hong Kong
U.S. & For Pat'd
Other Pat's
Pending
Hong Kong

The talking version of the Barbie® doll (stock #1195) had a short blonde shag hairdo, while Steffie (stock #1186) had long blonde hair with bangs. Both dolls also had rooted eyelashes and were marked:

© 1967
Mattel Inc.
U.S. & Foreign
Pats. Pend.
Hong Kong

The Ken® doll in this series was identical in every way to the non-talking doll except for his talking mechanism. Each of the Busy and Talking Busy dolls came with five brown plastic accessories: a telephone, a suitcase, a portable television, a carrying tray, and set of drinking glasses.

The last two new dolls produced by Mattel in 1972

BUSY KEN® IN TOWN TURTLE, STOCK #1430, CIRCA 1972.
The Busy Hands and Talking Busy Hands dolls were the last of Mattel's great body type innovations.

TALKING BUSY KEN® IN ORIGINAL OUTFIT.

TALKING BUSY STEFFIE AND TALKING BUSY BARBIE®, CIRCA 1972.
These two dolls had busy hands as well as talking mechanisms. Their limbs are very fragile and break off easily so finding either of these dolls intact is rare. The Talking Steffie is the first and only doll of that name to be produced as a blonde, while the Barbie® doll is one of the few to be produced with a shorter hairstyle. Both dolls have rooted eyelashes.
Steffie doll courtesy of Linda Oliva.

POSE N' PLAY TIFF IN SUPER SLACKS, STOCK #1736, CIRCA 1972.
Skipper doll's last Mod era friend was made from the same mold as Fluff but had auburn hair and a more flexible body.

POSE N' PLAY SKIPPER IN BEST BUY OUTFIT.
The last of the Mod era Skipper dolls had painted eyelashes and a poseable body.

were a Pose n' Play Skipper (stock #1179) and her friend Tiff (stock #1199). Both Pose n' Play Skipper and Tiff were similar in construction to the early Living dolls, but had new "swinging free" arms which allowed them further movement and poseability. Skipper had shoulder-length, strawberry-blonde hair with bangs and painted blue eyes, while Tiff, a tomboy, was made from the Fluff head mold and had straight, center-parted auburn hair and painted brown eyes. Their body markings were the same as those on Living Skipper.

JAPANESE FRANCIE IN FR2231 JAPANESE GOWN.
This is an example of a rare Mod era Francie and Francie outfit produced exclusively for the Japanese market.
Doll and outfit courtesy of Linda Oliva.

THE COLLECTIBLE ERA

1973 TO PRESENT

As previously stated, after 1972, Mattel seemed to try out a different gimmick to sell the Barbie® doll with each successive edition. There were dolls whose hair could be curled—the Quick Curl and Deluxe Quick Curl series— dolls with more mobility— Free Movin' series and Ballerina dolls—and many variations on the Malibu theme. For example, the 1976 Gold Medal Barbie® and Gold Medal Skater Barbie® were really the Malibu dolls in Olympic-themed sports outfits. There was also some attempt to update older dolls such as two versions of a trendier, long rooted hair Ken® doll—1973's Mod Hair Ken® and 1976's Now Look Ken®. There were also the well-intentioned but controversial Growing' Up Skipper and Ginger dolls which went through puberty with the twist of an arm. Two new friends were made from the Steffie mold: redheaded Kelley (available in both Quick Curl

A QUICK CURL BARBIE® IN ORIGINAL OUTFIT.
In the early 1970s, Mattel began to rely on gimmicks to sell dolls. This one has special hair that can be curled or straightened by using a special plastic curling wand.
Doll courtesy of Gene Foote.

BAGGIE CASEY (BRUNETTE) IN CHECK THIS, STOCK #1291, CIRCA 1973.
Francie's best friend made her last appearance as a budget "baggie" doll. Both the Baggie Francie and Baggie Casey had painted features, low-quality hair fibers, and straight arms and legs made of a flimsy plastic.

and Malibu-style Yellowstone editions) and African-American Cara (available as Free Movin', Quick Curl, and Ballerina dolls).

During the 1970s, Mattel focused on economy in order to keep rising toy costs down. Many older-edition dolls were also liquidated in simple plastic packages known as Baggie editions including the last two versions of Francie and Casey who had minimally painted faces, straight-legged, straight-waisted bodies and simple center-parted hairstyles.

The most notable change Barbie® and Ken® dolls underwent was in 1977 when both their faces were resculpted in an attempt to update them. Superstar Barbie® and Ken® could then fit in with the current disco scene with their flashy clothes, trendy hairstyles, and toothy grins. A black version of Superstar Barbie® called Superstar Christie was also available. There was also an 18-inch version of the Superstar Barbie® and Christie dolls called Supersize Barbie® which was available from 1977 to 1979. The Superstar Barbie® face mold proved to be so

MOD HAIR KEN® IN BEST BUY, STOCK #8617, CIRCA 1973.
This was the first rooted-hair Ken® doll to be put on the market. He also came with an array of flocked paper mustaches, sideburns, and beard pieces that could be stuck on by his owners.

SUPERSTAR BARBIE® DOLL IN ORIGINAL OUTFIT, CIRCA 1977.
Many collectors see this doll as the return to excellence in Mattel dolls. This is the face mold still being used on most dolls in production today.

SUPERSIZE SUPER HAIR BARBIE®, CIRCA 1978.
The final version of the 18-inch Supersize Barbie® doll produced by Mattel. This one has special Quick Curl hair. The 18-inch body has been used again recently for versions of Mattel's dolls based on Walt Disney animated characters such as Pocahontas and Esmeralda.

HISPANIC BARBIE®, CIRCA 1980.
The first Latina doll released by Mattel under the name Barbie® doll. Certain dolls are released in Hispanic editions in Spanish-speaking markets but, more recently, have been produced using the name of Barbie doll's Hispanic friend Teresa instead.

BLACK BARBIE®, CIRCA 1980.
The first African-American doll released under the name Barbie® doll. Today, most dolls are released in both black and white editions.

popular that it is still in use today on many Barbie® dolls.

Most of the play dolls created during the 1970s and into the 1980s are blonde-haired, blue-eyed, and differ from one another only in body mechanism or a change of outfit. Sadly, if not in their original packing and/or outfit, they are interchangeable and hardly memorable. The few exceptions include the Black and Hispanic versions of the

Barbie® doll produced in 1980. However, if you question the reduced quality or durability of the dolls from this period, it is important to remember that throughout the 1970s and 1980s, Mattel viewed its products solely as children's playthings, not long-term collectibles. However, this philosophy was to be altered in the next few years.

In 1980, Mattel started producing what turned out to

be their longest-running collector series, the International dolls (now called Dolls of the World). Due to the popularity of this series as well as awareness of adult collector interest through events such as the annual Barbie® Doll Collectors conventions, Mattel started to create new specialty and limited-edition dolls. Originally the market focus was on the general public but has since been targeted specifically to the more affluent adult collector. For example, originally Mattel produced lower-priced dolls made exclusively for department stores such as Sears and Walmart but the company has since expanded their market to include more expensive specialty dolls for such upscale venues as Bloomingdales, Macy's, and the toy store FAO Schwarz.

For this new market, Mattel has experienced a renaissance in creativity with new feats of hairstyling, costuming design and construction, and packaging. They have also

BOB MACKIE GOLD BARBIE® DOLL, CIRCA 1992.
The first doll in the very popular series designed by theatrical and fashion designer Bob Mackie. Although moderately priced when she was first released, this doll has become one of the hottest and most asked-for dolls by Barbie® doll collectors.

GREAT ERAS EGYPTIAN QUEEN BARBIE® DOLL, NEVER REMOVED FROM THE BOX, CIRCA 1994.
She was one of the second two releases in the highly collectible Great Eras series featuring dolls dressed in historical costumes. This doll was designed by collector favorite and veteran designer Carol Spencer.

SEARS BLOSSOM BEAUTIFUL BARBIE® DOLL, NEVER REMOVED FROM THE BOX, CIRCA 1992.
This was one of two dolls released as Sears Department Store Specials that year. It was supposed to be the first in a series of higher-priced dolls, but no others were ever produced. In fact, the following year, there was no Sears exclusive doll at all released in the United States, as Sears and Roebuck tried to restructure their company. She is highly collectible because many collectors missed ordering her and not many were produced.

SERVICE MERCHANDISE BLUE RHAPSODY BARBIE® DOLL, NEVER REMOVED FROM THE BOX, CIRCA 1991.
This doll was the first ever produced as an exclusive for the Service Merchandise mail order/catalog stores. Most collectors didn't know about her and so she commands a high secondary market price.

highlighted their own inventive design team with a series of signature dolls known as the Classique Collection as well as invited renowned couturiers to create Barbie® doll editions. Such names include Bob Mackie, Anne Klein, Donna Karan, Christian Dior, Calvin Klein, Nicole Miller, and Ralph Lauren. Mattel has also begun to cater to ethnic markets with higher-priced dolls, created by designer Byron Lars, as well as the Fashion Savvy series, featuring dolls of color, produced in 1997.

In order to increase their market even further, Mattel began to utilize new sales techniques in the early 1990s. In addition to selling dolls through established channels such as toy, doll, and department stores, Barbie® dolls were now available through direct marketing via infomercials and telemarketing. This has proven so successful that Mattel now sells a number of dolls exclusively through their Barbie Collectibles™ telemarketing/direct marketing division. They have also recently established themselves on the world wide web where you can view a variety of new dolls including Internet specials such as the limited-edition brunette Midnight Waltz Barbie®.

Special editions of the Barbie® doll and her friends for foreign markets have been produced by Mattel since the mid-1960s. During the 1970s and 1980s, overseas production expanded and several other companies were granted licenses to produce the Barbie® doll in their countries including Takara and Bandai in Japan, the Young Corporation in Korea, and Estrela in Brazil. However, in the early 1990s, as the Barbie® doll's global popularity began to grow, Mattel chose to do away with most foreign licensees and

WAREHOUSE EXCLUSIVE SEASONS GREETINGS BARBIE® DOLL, NEVER REMOVED FROM THE BOX, CIRCA 1994.
An example of one of the many dolls released as Exclusives for one of three wholesale club stores in the United States: Price Club/Costco, BJ's, and Sam's. Many collectors don't see these dolls because they are not members of one of the three clubs or don't have access to one in their immediate geographic area. Some years, all three stores get the same doll; other years, they each get their own exclusive. Occasionally, they have gotten both.

WALT DISNEY WORLD REDHAIRED EVERGREEN PRINCESS BARBIE® DOLL, NEVER REMOVED FROM THE BOX, CIRCA 1994.
Every year, a huge Doll and Teddy Bear Festival is held at the Walt Disney World Resort in Orlando, Florida. Many doll and bear companies attend and release limited-edition dolls. This is an example of one of the Barbie® dolls that was offered. It is a redhaired variation of the Evergreen Princess Barbie® doll, the normal edition of which was blonde. This edition was limited to 1,500 pieces.

SODA FOUNTAIN SWEETHEART COCA COLA, CIRCA 1996.
This is the first in a series of dolls based on old Coca Cola advertising and targeted for collectors of both Barbie® dolls and Coca Cola memorabilia that was available only through Mattel's direct mail Barbie® Collectibles division. She sold out very quickly and is very hot on the secondary market.

FILIPINA ETHNIC BARBIE® DOLL, MADE BY THE RICHWELL COMPANY, PHILLIPPINES.
One of the joys of Barbie® doll collecting is finding unusual foreign issues. This is one of a series of dolls based on native Filipina outfits. They were very limited in number and extremely difficult to obtain.

produce Barbie® dolls of their own for these hot new markets as well as the more traditional markets of Western European countries and Canada where American-style dolls have always sold well. In addition, there have been some foreign dolls created exclusively for European stores, such as Hamleys in London and Blokkers in the Netherlands, as well as the Italian Gardaland and Disneyland Paris® theme parks.

In recent years, the Asian and Pacific markets have expanded rapidly as well.

TEEN COURTNEY, SKIPPER, AND NIKKI DOLLS WEARING FASHION AVENUE FASHIONS, CIRCA 1997.
In 1997, Barbie® doll's little sister Skipper grew up. Here she is with her two friends Courtney and Nikki. These three dolls were considered "play dolls" but are quickly becoming collector favorites because of their beauty and modern looks. All three dolls wear Fashion Avenue™ Fashions, a line of better-quality clothing for Barbie® doll.

HARLEY-DAVIDSON BARBIE® DOLL, TOYS R US EXCLUSIVE, CIRCA 1997.
A good example of cross marketing is this 1997 Harley-Davidson Barbie® doll which was targeted at both Barbie® doll and Harley-Davidson motorcycle memorabilia collectors.

Please note that the motorcycle is not included with the doll.

BARBIE® MILLICENT ROBERTS DOLL, CIRCA 1996.
In 1996, Mattel released the first in a signature series of dolls and outfits just for adult collectors. This is the first in the series, which came in a gift set. The closed-mouth, full-lipped mold is known as the "Mackie" face because it has been used on most of the Bob Mackie dolls and is a collector favorite. Most regular edition dolls in Japan are also made from this mold.

There has always been high demand for Barbie® dolls in Japan but now other countries such as Australia, India, Taiwan, Singapore, and the Philippines are also becoming Barbie® doll conscious. A wide variety of unusual and innovative dolls can be found in these countries and any collection would benefit from at least one. In most foreign markets, the Superstar face mold is used on the Barbie® doll. However, in Japan, the closed-mouth, full-lipped mold used on the Bob Mackie dolls is substituted on such common play-type dolls as Songbird Barbie®, Barbie® Style Barbie® and the dolls used in multiple

EXPRESSIONS OF INDIA, SOHNI PUNJAB DI, MADE BY THE LEO COMPANY.
This is one of a series of dolls created for the Indian market which features native costumes, jewelry, and styling.

doll gift sets such as the Travellin' Sisters set.

In addition to all the new dolls produced, Mattel has been producing reproduction nostalgic dolls since 1994. This is in response to demands from both vintage and newer Barbie® doll collectors. Vintage (1959–1972) Barbie® and family dolls and clothing are getting more and more difficult to obtain and as a result prices have soared. The nostalgic vinyl series is a way for collectors to own their favorite vintage dolls and outfits at a fraction of the cost of the originals; for example, the 1996 and 1997 reproduction editions of the American Girl Barbie® doll and the 1997 reproduction of the African-American Francie doll.

Enthusiasm for Barbie® doll collecting and sharing

information amongst collectors led to the creation of the Barbie® Doll Collectors Conventions. These annual gatherings have grown rapidly in attendance since 1980 with no upper limit in sight. Only a few years ago, Mattel held their own 35th Anniversary Festival for 1,500 participants at the Walt Disney World theme park in Orlando, Florida. The Barbie® Doll Collector Conventions serve as a forum for exchanging knowledge, meeting old friends and

PENN STATE UNIVERSITY CHEERLEADER, NEVER REMOVED FROM THE BOX, CIRCA 1997.
Part of the fun of collecting is the thrill of the hunt. In 1997, Mattel released 19 different editions of the Cheerleader doll, featuring the colors and team mascots of 19 separate universities. Different dolls were available in different areas, making it a challenge to collect the entire set.

IN THE LIMELIGHT BARBIE® DOLL DESIGNED BY BYRON LARS, CIRCA 1997.
One of the newest dolls to be released through the direct market Barbie Collectibles™ division. Mattel has begun to explore the African-American collectors' market with the release of several upscale dolls including this one designed by Byron Lars, one of the hottest couturier designers on Seventh Avenue today.

making new ones, and seeing the rarest of Barbie® doll items.

One of the most anticipated events at any convention is the unveiling of the exclusive convention souvenir doll. Since 1993, Mattel has had a hand in producing the souvenir dolls in conjunction with the host club. Another exciting event is viewing the doll competition. While vintage items are judged on

their rarity and condition, the dolls in the "handmade" categories are always feats of creativity, innovation, and artistry. These artist dolls have in part spawned a new dimension in Barbie® doll collecting as more and more people begin to collect these customized beauties. Whether or not these dolls will increase in value in the future is still unknown, but the range and depth of talent is staggering.

In conclusion, if the future is anything like the past, the collectible Barbie® dolls in 30 years may be those the children of today love as friends rather than limited-edition specialty dolls.

GRAND PREMIÈRE CLUB DOLL, CIRCA 1997.
The first ever doll created exclusively for Mattel's official Barbie® doll Collectors Club, launched in 1997. Members received a special pin, membership card, newsletter subscription, limited edition Barbie® Millicent Roberts outfit, and the option to buy one of these exclusive dolls.

BARBIE® AND THE HONEY BEATS, A CONVENTION COMPETITION ENTRY FROM THE BARBIE® AND THE BANDSTAND CONVENTION BY THE AUTHOR.
An example of one of the winning dioramas created for a "handmade" division at the 1996 Barbie doll collectors convention in Philadelphia. The diorama placed second in the "Girl Groups" category.

**BANDSTAND BEAUTY BARBIE®
(CHAIRMAIN'S EDITION) AND
BANDSTAND BEAU.**
This doll is a variation on the blonde souvenir doll given out at the 1996 Philadelphia Barbie® and the Bandstand Barbie® doll collectors convention. Designed by doll artist Dick Tahsin, this special redhaired edition was limited to 14 pieces. Her companion is a limited-edition doll created for sale as a convention souvenir. Only 96 pieces were created and they were very much in demand by the end of the event.

RESOURCES

MATTEL

Barbie® Collectibles Division:
1-800-388-2266 or reachable on
the World Wide Web at
www.barbie.com
*Direct purchasing and customer
relations.*

PUBLICATIONS

Barbie® Bazaar—**The Barbie®
Collectors' Magazine**
Murat-Caviale, Inc.
5617 Sixth Avenue
Kenosha, Wisconsin 53140
Bi-monthly publication.

Miller's Guide
P.O. Box 8722
Spokane, Washington 99203-0722
*Quarterly publication featuring the
Barbie® doll as well as other collectible
fashion dolls.*

SHOWS

**Australian Barbie® Doll
Collectors Convention**
10 Coverly Court, Eaton,
WA 6230, Australia
*Annual event held in Sydney,
Australia.*

Doll Shows & Sales
F&M Promotions
P.O. Box 220
Fair Lawn, NJ 07410
*A series of all-Barbie® doll shows and
sales held several times a year on the
East Coast.*

Barbie® in Holland Convention
Ger Van Kempen
Livingstonelaan 520
3526 JC Utrecht
The Netherlands
31 30 802 110 (phone/fax)
Annual event held in the Netherlands.

**Convention for Barbie® Doll
Collectors**
Anita and Robert Weininger
01149-9187-8251 (phone/fax)
Annual event held in Germany.

**Eastern States Doll, Toy &
Teddy Bear Show & Sale**
The Maven Company, Inc.
P.O. Box 1538
Waterbury, CT 06721
203-758-3880
*New England's largest indoor doll, toy,
and teddy bear show held every spring
and fall at "The Big E" Center, West
Springfield, Massachussetts.*

**The Greater Northwest Doll
Show and Sale, Featuring the
Barbie® Doll**
Scott Arend
6319 24th Avenue NW #1
Seattle, WA 98107

**International Barbie®
Convention**
Martha and Wolfgang Bodenbach
Bachweg 36
56072 Koblenz, Germany
49 0261-26769 (phone/fax)

The Joe & Marl Shows
Joe Blitman
213-953-6490 or
Marl Davidson
941-751-6275
*A series of fashion doll shows and
sales held several times a year in
different parts of the country.*

**Motor City Barbie®
Mini-Convention**
Presented by the Great Lakes
Chapter Barbie® Doll Collector
Club
Contact: Dorinda Balanecki,
Chairperson
810-391-2242
*Annual event with proceeds donated
to charity.*

Paris Fashion Doll Festival
Kathy Moreau
9 Rue du Bois de l'Eglise
77280 Othis, France
33-1-60-03-2059 (phone)
33-1-60-03-4224 (fax)
Contact about future shows.

**S.U.N.Y. Stony Brook Burn
Center Doll, Toy & Teddy Bear
Show & Sale**
Sophie Mahoney
P.O. Box 1
Northport, NY 11768
516-261-6242
*Annual event with proceeds donated to
Stony Brook University Burn Center
Unit.*

AUCTIONS

McMaster's Auctions
P.O. Box 1755
Cambridge, OH 43725
614-432-4419 (Joyce at the Barbie
Auction Hotline)
614-432-3191 (fax)
*Holds two to three auctions a year
featuring Barbie® dolls, clothing, and
accessories.*

Scherzer's Mail Auction
Lisa Scherzer
54 Gates Court
Matawan, NJ 07747
908-290-1407
*Contact for future Barbie® doll mail
auctions.*

GENERAL
INFORMATION

Miniatures by Rebecca Brosdahl
7625 Lee Avenue North
Brooklyn Park, Minnesota 55443

BIBLIOGRAPHY

AMUDSEN, JOAN, AND LEONARD PLANES; *A Detailed Listing and Value Guide to Barbie® Doll Fashions, Volume 1;* Joan Amudsen, Plainview, New York, 1982

AMUDSEN, JOAN, AND LEONARD PLANES; *A Detailed Listing and Value Guide to Barbie® Doll Fashions, Volume 2;* Joan Amudsen, Plainview, New York, 1984

BLITMAN, JOE; *Vive la Francie;* Joe Blitman, Los Angeles, California, 1992

BLITMAN, JOE; *Barbie® Doll & her Mod, Mod, Mod, Mod World of Fashion (1967–1972);* Hobby House Press, Grantsville, Maryland 1996

BLITMAN, JOE; *Barbie® Doll's Cousin Francie & her Mod, Mod, Mod, Mod World of Fashion;* Hobby House Press, Grantsville, Maryland, 1996

BRYAN, SANDRA; *Barbie®: The Eyelash Era Fashions 1967–1972;* Sandra Bryan, Houston, Texas, 1989

BRYMAN, SANDRA; *Ken® Fashions 1961–1976;* Sandra Bryan, Houston, Texas, 1990

BOY, BILLY; *Barbie®: Her Life and Times;* Crown Publishing, New York, 1987

DAVIDSON, MARL B; *Barbie® Doll Structures and Furniture;* Hobby House Press, Grantsville, Maryland, 1997

DEUTSCH, STEFANIE; *Barbie®: The First 30 Years—1959 through 1989;* Collectors Books, Paducah, Kentucky, 1996

DEWEIN, SYBIL, AND JOAN ASHABRANER; *The Collectors' Encyclopedia of Barbie® Dolls and Collectibles;* Collectors Books, Paducah, Kentucky, 1977

DEWEIN, SYBIL ST. JOHN; *Collectible Barbie® Dolls, 1977–1967;* Mrs. Sybil St. John DeWein, Clarksville, Tennessee, 1980

EAMES, SARAH SINK; *Barbie® Fashion Volume 1, 1959 to 1967;* Collectors Books, Paducah, Kentucky, 1990

EAMES, SARAH SINK; *Barbie® Fashion Volume 2, 1967 to 1974;* Collectors Books, Paducah, Kentucky, 1997

FAROANE, JIM; *Fashion Doll Makeovers;* Hobby House Press, Grantsville, Maryland, 1996

FENNICK, JANINE; *The Collectible Barbie® Doll;* Running Press, Philadelphia, 1996

HANDLER, RUTH, WITH JACQUELINE SHANNON; *Dream Doll: The Ruth Handler Story;* Longmeadow Press, Stamford, Connecticut, 1994

LORD, M.G.; *Forever Barbie®: The Unauthorized Biography of a Real Doll;* William A. Morrow & Co., New York, 1994

MANDEVILLE, A. GLENN; *Contemporary Doll Stars;* Hobby House Press, Grantsville, Maryland, 1992

MANDEVILLE, A. GLENN; *Doll Fashion Anthology and Price Guide;* Hobby House Press, Grantsville, Maryland, 1987

MANOS, SUSAN AND PARIS; *The World of Barbie® Dolls;* Collectors Books, Paducah, Kentucky, 1983

MANOS, SUSAN AND PARIS; *The Wonder of Barbie® Dolls;* Collectors Books, Paducah, Kentucky, 1987

PILKENTON, LINDA; *Skipper Fashion Value Guide 1964–1976;* Sandra Bryan, Austin, Texas, 1990

RANA MARGO; *Barbie® Doll Exclusives;* Collectors Books, Paducah, Kentucky, 1995

SHIBANO, KEIKO, KIMURA; *Barbie® Doll in Japan;* Murat Caviale, Kenosha, Wisconsin, 1994

STERN, JANE AND MICHAEL; *Sixties People;* Alfred A. Knopf, New York, 1990

The author, Janine Fennick, looks forward to hearing from fellow Barbie® doll collectors and enthusiasts. She can be reached by mail at: P.O. Box 9, Commack, NY 11725 or by e-mail at JanAtJaime@aol.com. She is also always interested in adding old and unusual items to her collection.

INDEX